Praise for Fulfilled

I have never met such an amazing woman of God as Danise Jurado. The way she lives her life, the compassion she has for others, and the excellence that is exemplified in everything that she does is such an inspiration to me. Her new book, *Fulfilled*, is a wake-up call to the body of Christ, no matter where they are in their walk with God. I believe this book will change so many lives, and I can't wait to see just how much God will bless it.

Pastor Matthew Barnett
Co-founder of The Dream Center and Senior Pastor of Angelus Temple

Danise Jurado has been an integral part of The Dream Center and Angelus Temple for many years. She approaches ministry with great knowledge of Scripture and boldness, as well as gentleness and vulnerability. Danise has an incredible passion for counseling and will stop at nothing to see people obtain wholeness through Christ. I have been impacted by her teaching, preaching, and love for God and His people. As you will read, Danise has gone through many challenges in her life, but has always chosen to allow those challenges to deepen her faith. This book is a true gift to any reader as it contains wisdom to face many of life's circumstances.

Caroline Barnett
Co-pastor of The Dream Center and Angelus Temple

As a person who has worked in the health and fitness industry for over twenty-two years, I believe in full mind, body, and spirit wellness. I teach people how to eat well and how to get into shape. The spiritual component is very important. This book *Fulfilled* will add that component. The way Danise teaches you to read the Word of God, get close to God, to trust God and walk in complete freedom are life changing. I highly recommend this book.

Christine Avanti-Fischer
Bestselling author, Skinny Chicks Eat Real Food *(Rodale 2012)*

Fulfilled

DANISE JURADO

LEARNING TO LIVE
THE LIFE
GOD PROMISED

N|T NEWTYPE

Fulfilled
Copyright © 2015, Danise Jurado

ISBN-10: 1942306105
ISBN-13: 978-1942306108

Publisher's Cataloging-in-Publication data

Jurado, Danise.
    Fulfilled : Learning to Live the Life God Promised / Danise Jurado.
    pages cm
    ISBN 978-1942306108

1. Christian life. 2. God. 3. Self-actualization (Psychology) --Religious aspects. 4. Spiritual life. I. Title.

BL624 .J87 2015
248.4 --dc23   2015909069

Published by NEWTYPE Publishing
newtypepublishing.com

Thank you to Midpoint (distributor):

Chris & Karen Bell   Nicholas Sinisi
Midpoint Trade Books   Midpoint Trade Books
15964 Parklane   27 West 20th Street
Northville, MI 48168   Suite 1102
                              New York, NY 10011

Editorial services by SplitSeed, *www.Split-Seed.com*
Book Design by Pam Terry, *www.Opus1Design.com*
Cover Design by John Esparza, @JohnSparz, *www.EsparzaCreative.com*

Printed in the United States of America
First Edition

N|T NEWTYPE

To my husband, Kurt,
and our children and grandchildren.

Live Fulfilled.

Contents

Our Need for God

I'm kneeling. Tears are streaming down my face. They come from deep inside me—a place no one sees, sometimes not even me. Except for Him. He always sees. His compassion gently lifts the layers I have built. I have come to Him, needing all that He has to offer. It's my favorite place because I am safe here. In the arms of unconditional love, He challenges me to be more than I think I can be. He gives me strength, and there is resolve in my heart. I stand, ready to take the next step. His wisdom guides my path as I walk the road He has marked out. He never leaves my side, and peace fills my heart. He patiently redirects me when I have misunderstood His plan. He always has just the right words for me. I begin to see glimpses of Him in me. One step at a time, I walk with Him. As days turn into weeks, then months and years pass by, I understand my need for Him in ways I never did before.

I look into the eyes of people around me. I see the hope that is trying to live in their hearts. They notice a reflection of Him in me and ask, "Can you help me?" Although I feel inadequate, He is there and always ready to help. They say, "We want to believe. We want to believe that He really loves us, *but*...." Such a little word and yet it places limits when He has none. Pain has given them reason to be guarded, but His hope replaces all discouragement. His truth is always enough to bring the freedom we need, as He loves us in personal ways that only He can. One by one, we come to God, young and old, wealthy and homeless; not one of us is alike. Yet we are the same, we're all learning to live the life God promised and longing to be fulfilled.

On any given day, the multitudes of anxieties within us carve out places in our hearts needing to be filled. There is a pang inside of us desiring to be truly satisfied and free from the heavy weights holding us down. Just as our bodies need sleep, nourishment, and exercise; our soul longs to be filled. This yearning to be whole and complete cannot be ignored. If we try to deny it, we'll only be tempted to find fulfillment in ways that ultimately disappoint us further. Temporary distractions offered by the world around us can only satisfy on the surface. They are counterfeits for the powerful, life-changing promises that can only be found in God. In the midst of all the anxieties we face, He is standing at the door of our heart; God is knocking. Can you hear Him? It is the soft sound of His compassion. God extends His hand to us, ready to lead us into our divine destiny. His promises are great and precious nourishment to our souls. We find them by responding to His invitation and receiving the words He has spoken to us in the Bible. No matter where we are in our spiritual life, God is reaching out to us with His truth. As we partner with Him, we soon discover that spiritual freedom is a powerful reality that will revive our numbness, heal the brokenness, and fill every void.

As I sit in my office at The Dream Center where I've served as an assisting pastor for the past fourteen years, I look into the eyes of those sitting across from me. Life can be so difficult, sometimes even brutal and dark. It takes a toll on the heart, mind, and soul. They are searching for peace, hope, freedom...help. My heart breaks as I see the depths of their personal pain, and my heart jumps for joy as I witness their restoration. We walk together from spiritual emptiness to fulfillment through Jesus Christ, our Lord. The hidden potential that God has placed within us lies just beneath the surface in our lives. Empowered by the Word of God and presence of His Spirit, that potential emerges through freedom into our destined purpose.

Betrayal, loss, addiction, hopelessness, abuse, fear, and doubt whisper, "Is a fulfilled life even possible? How?" God has the answers we search for. His wisdom unlocks the mystery and helps us discover the fulfilled life He promised.

CHAPTER I

Forgiveness

"But you are a forgiving God, gracious and compassionate, slow to anger and abounding in love."

NEHEMIAH 9:17

From the first moment God introduced Himself to me and through every step of life since then, His compassion and forgiveness have captivated my heart. Learning to live with a heart full of forgiveness is quite possibly the most challenging, yet spiritually freeing, quality we can learn from God.

For the first twenty-one years of my life, I was completely unaware of how spiritually empty I was. I didn't know how genuinely satisfied my soul could be until I met Him. God helped me discover everything I never knew I needed, beginning with forgiveness.

I was raised in a loving home, but we never went to church. I never attended worship services, Sunday school class, youth group meetings, or camp. I never read the Bible. I believed in God, but my belief was in the image of who I thought God was. I never took the time to allow God the opportunity to define and introduce Himself to me through the pages of the Bible. Looking back, there was a lot I didn't understand, but that didn't matter to God. His love and mercy collided with my ignorance and pride, and I was changed forever.

The story I am about to share with you might sound radical to some; to others, it may seem completely normal; but for me, it was the moment I met the one true, living God, the day Christ found me, and I accepted Him into my heart. Although decades have passed since then, the powerful impact God made in my life is forever vivid in my memory. The year was 1987, and I had the big hair to prove it.

At the time, my mom had just recently become a Christian and started attending church. It was a very small congregation. They met in an old, run-down building located in the middle of California's High Desert. I went to visit my mom and purposefully planned to arrive later on that Sunday morning to avoid going to church with her. This new "church thing" in my mom's life was okay for her, but I didn't have any desire for it.

When I got to her house, she was still at church, so I thought, "I'll just sit in the back of the church and wait for her." I walked into the church about an hour and a half after the service started, and it was still going. That's an understatement. They were still going, all right. Nothing could have prepared me for what I was about to see. As I walked into the back of the church, I saw men and women jumping up and down, shouting hallelujah, and flailing their arms; everyone was talking, but I couldn't understand what anyone was saying. There were two men at the front of church praying for people. I quietly sat in the back with my arms folded, literally rolling my eyes in judgment. "These people can't be serious," I thought. Then, I remember actually being concerned for my mom, concluding, "Oh, my gosh, my mom is involved in a cult. Weird, desert cult people have brainwashed my mom!"

My criticism grew as I saw people falling to the ground and others catching them. I just sat there, minding my own judgmental business, when one of the men, in the middle of praying for someone, stopped suddenly. He turned around, pointed at me, and said, "I need to pray for you." My eyes widened like a deer caught in headlights as I shook my head back and forth, uttering, "Ah, no, no you don't." A few minutes later, I couldn't take it any longer, so I stood up and left. I didn't just walk out; I ran out of the back of that church as fast as I could.

I didn't know at the time that the men who were praying for people were traveling evangelists. The senior pastor of the church was actually sitting in the back, so when I barreled out the doors of his church, he followed me. He met me outside and tried to explain to me what I had seen. The pastor was a very kind yet bold and confident person. He hinted that if I had a problem with what was happening in the church service, then my problem was with Jesus. Humoring him, I answered, "I know that you don't know me, but I am a good person." The pastor looked me in the eyes with kindness and gently replied, "You might be a good person, but without Jesus, you are a good person going straight to hell." Then he turned and walked away, leaving me to think about what he had said. As I pondered the pastor's words, there was a part of me that wanted to be offended by his statement; however, I could tell that he wasn't personally attacking me. He genuinely believed what he was telling me, which I found intriguing.

I decided to go back into the church and find out more. As I quietly re-entered and took a seat in the back, my heart pounded so hard it felt like it was going to jump out of my chest. I wasn't there even five minutes when one of the evangelists pointed me out again saying, "I need to pray for you." This time, I got up. As I began walking up the aisle toward the front of the church, I wasn't thinking about God at all. I was wearing a new white outfit, and I had noticed the old tile floor of the church seemed dirty to me. All the way up the aisle, I thought to myself, "There is *no* way I am falling down on this dirty floor like the rest of these fools!" I was determined. I continued to prepare myself, "I don't care if this guy pushes me; I am *not* going down!" Even when we aren't thinking about God, He is always thinking about us.

Once I reached the front, the evangelist gently placed his fingertips on my forehead and began praying over me. The next thing I knew, I was on the floor. When God shows up in your life, believe me, you know it. My hands were covering my face. In that moment, I knew that God was real, and He touched me. No sermon was preached, and no one led me in the sinner's prayer, yet tears welled in my eyes as I realized my sin for the first time. The recognition of my sin seemed to be magnified in contrast to the holiness I felt from God. I knew deep in my heart that I was in the presence of pure holiness, and although I was very aware of my sin, I felt God's love and compassion for me at the same time. My soul was renewed and revived. Tears were now freely flowing as I experienced God's unbelievable love and forgiveness for me.

For the first time in my life, I had a genuinely clean slate, and it was amazing. I walked into that church skeptical, critical, and prideful, but I left a brand new person with the hope of unconditional love. That was my very first taste of spiritual fulfillment and the beginning of my life in so many ways. I never could have imagined on that day, nearly thirty years ago, that I would actually become a minister and be given the opportunity to help others discover the same fulfilled life God has promised to them.

WE ALL NEED FORGIVENESS

*"Indeed, there is no one on earth who is righteous,
no one who does what is right and never sins."*

ECCLESIASTES 7:20

The topic of sin has become so needlessly controversial. It's really quite simple; we're human. We all equally stand on the common ground of humanity and are in need of God's forgiveness for our sins. Sometimes we find ourselves filled with regret because of our mistakes. Regret is the internal sting of sin. The revelation of our human tendency to sin should be the uniting catalyst that propels us all to a greater understanding of our personal need for God. Instead of uniting us, the topic of sin has become saturated with personal opinions that have caused division among us. Our sin cannot be defined by comparing ourselves with others, but rather in comparing ourselves to God's standard. When humanity is compared to the perfection of God, we are all found guilty.

*"Everyone who believes in him receives
forgiveness of sins through His name."*

ACTS 10:43

The weight of a guilty conscience creates a barrier between us and God that He never intended for us to have. Shame builds a wall against the love God has for us. He desires for each of us to experience a confident relationship with Him. God has torn down every barrier and wall our sin has built. Forgiveness is the very key to our salvation through Christ Jesus. It clears our guilty conscience, giving us a fresh start. With a clear conscience, we are liberated and become a pure vessel for the Holy Spirit.

Receiving and Extending Forgiveness

"Be kind and compassionate to one another, forgiving each other, just as in Christ God forgave you."

Ephesians 4:32

Receiving forgiveness is truly wonderful. God only asks that we share with others what He has so graciously already given to us. That almost makes it sound easy to do, but it's not. Sometimes the pain others have caused us can leave us wondering if we can ever forgive them for what they have done. The memories of the offense replay in our minds as we build our case against them. We convince ourselves that their offense doesn't warrant our forgiveness. Quite possibly, they don't deserve our forgiveness, but then, we should ask ourselves, does our behavior justify God's forgiveness extended to us?

"He does not treat us as our sins deserve or repay us according to our iniquities."

Psalm 103:10

God doesn't hold grudges. His forgiveness is complete. He treats us with the same love and forgiveness on our bad days as He does on our good days. Even when our behavior doesn't deserve it, God extends his mercy and gives us chance after chance for redemption. When our hearts are filled with gratitude to God for forgiving us, it is much easier to forgive others from the overflow of our hearts. Although the behavior of others might not deserve our forgiveness, God has equipped us to extend the same mercy He has shown to us.

Throughout the pages of this book, I will vulnerably share my own personal stories of addiction, betrayal, and painful disappointments. Each of these difficult experiences led me to discover my underlying need to extend forgiveness to others and myself. Learning how to forgive became the foundation for greater restoration in my life.

When we extend forgiveness to others, we aren't saying that what they did is okay. We are admitting that we have been wronged or hurt. When God forgives us, He is not saying that what we did was okay or that he approved of our behavior. He forgives us through Christ because it is His nature to love and forgive. We can't give what we don't have to give. When we accept God's forgiveness, we also receive the nature of God within us. We have been given the powerful love of God to forgive others too.

Forgiving others actually frees our soul. As we release others from the consequences of their offenses against us, we also release the spiritual and emotional burdens that we carried while we harbored an unforgiving attitude.

I Thought I Already Forgave Them

Realizing my need to extend forgiveness was a process that I didn't embrace easily. The easier solution seemed to be to forget and move on. In the next chapter, I'll share my full story of both forgiveness and restoration, but for now, it's enough to say that I eventually discovered that the "stuff it" approach doesn't work long term. After having some temporary success, out of nowhere I would be jolted again with the emotional pain that was still trapped in my heart. It always seemed to be triggered by simple things; a certain song or a specific smell could bring all the hurt flooding to the surface again. God began to show me that true forgiveness is so much more than just simply forcing hurtful memories out of my mind.

How do we know whether or not we have forgiven someone? We need to pay close attention to our actions; they will
eventually reveal deeper truths. Specifically, when we are
under stress, unhealthy behavior patterns can surface, and
often these are little warning signs to let us know that we have
some unresolved business in our hearts looking for a way out.

Bitterness that has been held in our hearts can come out
in a lot of different ways. It can be as subtle as uncharacteristic
moodiness or as extreme as panic attacks, depending on the
depth of the offense that has been buried. Over the years as a
pastoral counselor, I have walked the forgiveness journey with
many people trying to overcome violent trauma, such as mental, physical, and sexual abuse. In these situations, the unset-
tled pain can even reveal itself through physical symptoms,
such as stomach problems and skin rashes, addictive behaviors, or nightmares. Extending forgiveness is actually more for
our benefit than for the people we are choosing to forgive.

Our hearts are not designed to harbor excessive amounts
of pain and offense. Picture, for a moment, in your mind a
dam. There is a huge wall holding back enormous amounts
of water. The water levels in a dam must be monitored. If the
levels become too high, the dam is in danger of overflowing
or worse, completely breaking down. Spillways and pressure
release valves are used to relieve the dam and provide a healthy
exit strategy for the extra water. In the same way, offenses
that we have not dealt with will pile up in our hearts, creating
emotional and spiritual pressure. Forgiveness gives the pain a
healthy exit strategy to leave our hearts. If we don't give the
pain a healthy exit strategy, it will find an unhealthy way out.
Normally, this leads to some kind of destruction, either to ourselves, those around us, or both. The solution is to temporarily

revisit the offense. The key word here is *temporarily*. The goal is not to live in the past, only to reconnect with any offense that hasn't been dealt with, and then, intentionally and purposefully, release the pain of the offense with the help of Christ.

FORGIVENESS HOMEWORK

Although it is difficult, with God's help we are able to forgive. Even the offenses we thought we would never let go of can be forgiven. Completely forgiving someone can be a lengthy process. The first step begins with a choice. In the beginning moments of making this choice, we are not really sure how we will forgive, but we are at least willing. There is no limit to what God can do with a willing heart.

Next, we have to make a commitment to do daily forgiveness homework. You might be thinking, "Homework? What is forgiveness homework?" It is a very practical tool that has helped me to let go of the bitterness in my own heart and, over the years, proven to assist many others discover freedom. These steps create an intentional partnership with God to release all offenses and any built up resentment, anger, and bitterness. These kind of emotions don't just go away over time or on their own. Left unattended, they burrow themselves deep into our soul and begin to form our identity and affect our behaviors.

The soul is designed to need God. These are tried and true steps to forgiveness; implementing them will begin to liberate your soul in powerful and life-changing ways. Many people think that they don't need homework, or they feel that there isn't any amount of homework that could possibly work. Believe me, I've heard all the skeptical debates before.

Using these steps, I've helped many overcome some of life's most difficult and painful traumas. I can confidently tell you that this process works. To the extent that one is willing to surrender, Jesus has a 100% success rate in healing.

The first day will be the lengthiest part of the forgiveness homework. After that, it will literally only take you under a minute to do every day. On the first day, begin with a blank sheet of paper. Across the top of the page, write out this sentence:

FORGIVENESS HOMEWORK

"I forgive (name of one person who has hurt you) for _____ in the name of Jesus, and I bless (name of person who has hurt you) in the name of Jesus."

- _____
- _____
- _____

The most important part of this homework is to forgive and bless in the name of Jesus. Why do you have to bless them? You are not blessing them *because* they hurt you; rather, you are blessing them with more of Christ in their lives. Would you agree that the people who hurt you need more of Christ? In some situations, the people we need to forgive might have already passed away. When this is the case, you can change the wording from *bless* to *release*. Instead of forgiving and blessing them, you forgive and release them.

Underneath this sentence, use bullet points to create a detailed list of all the ways this person has hurt you. This list will fill in the blank section of your sentence, explaining the reasons you are offended or hurt. As you write your list, remember that the purpose is *not* to hold onto the hurt and build a stronger case against him or her. It is to release the pain of each offense one at a time and allow the love of Christ to fill that space in your heart instead. Depending on how long you have been holding on to these hurts and the depth of trauma they have caused, you might find that you are able to fill up an entire page or more with all the painful memories you have to let go of.

Try to avoid labeling the offense what you think others would call it. There is great importance in articulating how others' actions made you feel. Sometimes we excuse the painful memory and justify actions to help our mind let go of the hurt, but that doesn't heal the heart. There is no need to validate the hurt. That is one of the beautiful things about forgiveness homework—it's a personal partnership of healing with you and Jesus. He already knows the hurt is there, and He isn't asking for an explanation. God's desire is to heal and free you from the burdens.

Don't be surprised if God reveals a few other people to add to the list of those whom you need to forgive. Complete a new page for each person. Some will only have one offense written on the page, while others may have the entire front and back of the page covered. That's okay. Make sure to include a page for yourself if there are things from your past you have not forgiven yourself for. You can change the wording to "I receive all the blessings God has for me" instead of "I bless myself" since the latter sounds awkward to say. Depending on the circumstances, forgiving ourselves can be the hardest part of the homework.

Once you have your sentence and list of offenses written out, it's time to give it all to God. The most effective way to do this is to say this sentence out loud one time for each offense, filling in the blank with each offense until you get to the end of your list. Why do you have to say it out loud? There are two reasons: first, God has given you the power of life and death in your tongue (Proverbs 18:21). Second, faith establishes itself through hearing, so you will build your faith as you hear yourself speak forgiveness and blessing over this person (Romans 10:17).

This can be an extremely emotional exercise. It will help to close your eyes; put your hand over your heart; take a deep, cleansing breath; and repeat the name "Jesus, Jesus, Jesus" before and in between saying each sentence.

After the first day, your forgiveness homework is to say this simple sentence once each day: "I *forgive* (name of the person who has hurt you) in the name of *Jesus*, and I *bless* (name of person who has hurt you) in the name of *Jesus*." There is no need to continue daily repeating all the things you need to forgive them for. You already did that in complete detail on day one.

How long will you have to do this forgiveness homework? It really depends on each situation. Sometimes, it can take a couple of days or a week, but sometimes, it can take a lot longer, especially if you are letting go of a very painful trauma. You'll know when you are done. One day, you will speak the forgiveness and blessing over those who have hurt you, and you will realize that the pain is gone. If you are willing and committed to do it for as long as it takes, you will slowly begin to see your heart soften and freedom replace the tight restraints of bitterness. Once the process of healing and freedom through forgiveness has started, God continues to bring healing in every area.

There are a few things I should prepare you for. It is common to feel a combination of emotions as you speak out your forgiveness every day. It might even feel like you have opened a flood of emotions you have no desire to feel. This is often the case when we have allowed a very deep hurt to burrow itself and grow roots of bitterness. Many of the people I have assisted in this process have a history of nightmares due to past trauma. These nightmares occasionally recur during the forgiveness process. If this happens, keeping a journal will help you partner with God as He lovingly reveals deeper pain that needs to be released through forgiveness.

The pain or anger might seem too big to handle. You might even feel like you aren't strong enough to deal with the pain, but don't give up on the homework. Your freedom and breakthrough are coming through this process of forgiving. You don't have to face this on your own. God is right there with you every step of the way. His love drives out all fear, He is your strength when you feel like you are at your weakest, and He is the healer of your heart.

> *"That is why, for Christ's sake, I delight in weaknesses…For when I am weak, then I am strong."*
> 2 CORINTHIANS 12:10

> *"He heals the brokenhearted and binds up their wounds."*
> PSALM 147:3

*"The LORD is close to the brokenhearted
and saves those who are crushed in spirit."*

Psalm 34:18

*"Be strong and courageous. Do not be afraid or
terrified, for the* Lord *your God goes with you;
he will never leave you nor forsake you."*

Deuteronomy 31:6

While doing the forgiveness homework, you might not feel any anxiety or pain at all; in fact, you may feel the exact opposite. The words of forgiveness might roll right off your tongue as though they mean nothing at all. In this case, you might recognize a little moodiness or even a little anger throughout your day. Understand that, even if you refuse to allow your emotions to engage with the words of forgiveness you are speaking, by speaking them, you have declared an end to your bitterness. This is not something our sin nature generally likes. The emotions will find a way to come out as you take a daily stand for your freedom.

By speaking forgiveness and blessing over those who have hurt us, we are daily drawing a line in the sand that says, "I refuse to live in the past! I press forward to discover all God has for me today!" God's love, healing, and strength will accompany you on the daily journey, and the blessing of freedom will be yours to enjoy.

Forgiveness Precedes Restoration

In addition to our own personal freedom and healing, there exists another compelling reason to forgive others: when we withhold forgiveness, it becomes our sin.

*"But if you do not forgive others their sins,
your Father will not forgive your sins."*
MATTHEW 6:15

I learned this in a very impactful way. I was at a mid-week church service, and I had been a Christian for only about four years. The service's topic was sin—not just any kind of sin, but specifically secret sin. This kind of sin might seem to go unnoticed, but it's there just the same. As the sermon progressed, I became convicted of secret sin in my life. The pastor closed the service differently than usual. He had all of us bow our heads in prayer; then, he excused the congregation, except for those who felt convicted of secret sin. He asked us to stay, so there I sat as everyone filed out of the church around me. I have to admit that I was feeling a little humiliated, and I wondered what everyone was thinking of me. I lifted my head up and was relieved to see that I wasn't the only "secret sinner" in the church. The pastor led us in a personal prayer of confession. I prayed that night and confessed to God that my secret sin was unforgiveness and bitterness. I had justified my bitterness and denied that it was a sin for so long. It was a huge breakthrough for me just to confess that unforgiveness was a sin.

*"If we confess our sins, he is faithful and just
and will forgive us our sins and purify us
from all unrighteousness."*
1 JOHN 1:9

God doesn't need us to confess our sins because He already knows what they are. He asks us to confess because when we humble ourselves and admit our sins to Him, we open the door to our healing and renewal.

The person I was holding bitterness toward was my husband. God desired to redeem and restore my marriage, and I was about to learn firsthand that forgiveness always precedes restoration.

CHAPTER 2

Restoration

*"Every valley shall be filled in,
every mountain and hill made low.
The crooked road shall become straight,
the rough ways smooth."*

LUKE 3:5

It's difficult to feel complete when your life is filled with broken pieces. God mends the shattered fragments through the beautiful and sometimes painful process of restoration. My life's love story is also a story of restoration. At the time this book is released, my husband, Kurt, and I will have been married for twenty-nine years. We are a living testimony that God redeems lives, marriages, and relationships. We met and fell in love during high school. He was on the wrestling team, and I was a cheerleader. We didn't attend church, and although we believed that there was a God, we didn't yet understand what it meant to live for Him. We had all the typical, teenage ups and downs in our relationship that accompany growing up and learning about adulthood. There were two consistent things in our lives at that time: our love for each other and Kurt's social drinking. At that time, Kurt was always the life of the party, and his drinking just seemed to be teenage fun. As we grew up and finished high school, it became obvious that his drinking wasn't just teenage fun anymore—it was a lifestyle. His motto was "work hard, party harder." I told myself, "It's not that bad; lots of people drink. He works hard all week, so it's okay if he wants to party on the weekends." We got married, and in many ways, it seemed like we were well on our way to building our life together. However, his weekend partying eventually became out-of-control alcohol binges and a growing concern. I began to realize that it wasn't just a harmless lifestyle; Kurt's drinking was, quite obviously, an adult problem. Slowly, I came to terms with the fact that my husband was an alcoholic.

I remember that I dreaded Fridays. I never knew if he would come home from work. Most Friday and Saturday nights, he would stay out drinking all night long. I wouldn't hear from him until he came home drunk in the early morning hours. Then, he began drinking and staying out during the week too. We had only been married six months, and I was seriously considering a divorce. I was about to discover that God had a different plan.

It was at this point in my life that I visited that small church, the one I mentioned in the last chapter, and I experienced God's love for the first time. That day, I gave my whole heart to God, but I didn't know anything about the Bible or about being a Christian. I only understood the basic concepts—God loves me, forgives me, and saves me from sin through His Son, Jesus. With each day, I grew closer to God, and He quickly became my best friend and confidant. I talked to God all the time and read the Bible to find answers to the questions I had. The number one question on my mind in those days was, "What should I do with my marriage?" It didn't take me long to find out God's opinion regarding the covenant of marriage. However, my dilemma remained the same: I was married to a man I truly loved, and he loved his addiction.

As I remember some of my prayers during that time, I can see that they were laced with everything from selfish motives to complete desperation. Sometimes I would pray, "God, I am yours, but you know that I came to you as a package deal, so *change my husband!*" Other times, the process was so painful I would plead with God to release me from my marriage. God's answer always remained the same, "Pray for your husband." I was a brand new Christian, and I didn't have a lot of knowledge, but I knew that there was a spiritual battle going on for our marriage and, more importantly, for my husband. Little by little, God taught me how to truly intercede for Kurt in prayer.

When It Rains, It Pours

When you are walking through the restoration process with God, it tends to be a turbulent road all on its own. Often, life will give us quite a bit more than we think we can handle. The first few years of my Christian walk with God were some of the most difficult times I have faced in my life. I continued to pray to God for Kurt's victory, but at the time, his addiction was winning most of the battles.

It seems that our most challenging seasons in life are accompanied by unexpected crisis moments. It's as though we are doing all we can to emotionally hold on, and then, out of the blue, we are hit with more bad news. It was late in the afternoon when I got the call no one ever wants to receive. My fourteen-year-old brother, Chip, was in an accident. He was unconscious and in the intensive care unit (ICU) at the hospital. Kurt and I raced to be at his bedside with my family. We spent days watching and praying in my brother's ICU room. Chip never regained consciousness. His injuries were fatal. I was holding his hand when the nurse looked up at me and said, "I am so sorry. He's gone." All the prayers and faith I could muster up weren't enough; he was gone. Just months before his accident, my brother accepted Christ Jesus into his life. He had experienced some dark times leading up to his salvation, but at his memorial service, many reminisced about the last time they saw Chip and how he was sharing the hope of God with them. It was beautiful to see the hope of God alive in people during a time of such brokenness and loss.

Not long after my brother passed away, I experienced two miscarriages, and my stepfather was diagnosed with terminal cancer. Devastation, hopelessness, and pain seemed to be surrounding me. In the midst of the dark circumstances in my life, God's faithful promises encouraged me through. One day I cried out to God, "Lord it really seems like my life has fallen apart ever since I gave it to you." I remembered the scripture God gave to me after my brother died. Promise reached down to a deep place in my heart and brought me hope.

> *"I have told you these things, so that in me you may*
> *have peace. In this world you will have trouble.*
> *But take heart! I have overcome the world."*
>
> John 16:33

Life is filled with challenges and, sometimes, real trouble. Unfortunately, heartbreak and loss are an inevitable part of life. I realized that I would have faced all those trials either way, but God saved me just in time so that I would not have to face them alone. God is a very present help and great source of peace in our times of trouble.

THE UPS AND DOWNS
ON THE ROAD TO RESTORATION

During those few days in my brother's hospital room, Kurt called out to God and prayed for revelation, and God answered him with a very special and personal vision. Kurt's faith in God grew and inspired him to make efforts to change. Restoration is often an up and down process. He would take a few steps forward in faith only to fall again as his addiction kept holding him back.

I spent many nights praying for Kurt as his binges continued to get worse. Three or four times a week, he would be out until the early morning hours. I never knew who he was out with or where he was. I knew that he had been either drinking, doing drugs, or both because, when he finally did come home, he was too intoxicated to walk straight or talk without slurring his words. He would often attend church with me, and I would see glimpses of freedom in him. Other times, he would be too hung over to get out of bed. I continued to hold on to the hope I found in God.

"For we live by faith, not by sight."
2 CORINTHIANS 5:7

In spite of the underlying condition of our marriage at the time, we both really wanted to start a family. Discouraged by the previous miscarriages, I was afraid that I would never have children. When our son, Nicholas, was born, he brought such happiness and hope to us. I have to admit that there was a part of me hoping that Kurt's love for our son and his genuine desire to be a good dad would help him change his drinking habits. Down deep, I knew it was going to take more than that. As our son grew from an infant to a toddler, so did Kurt's drinking problem.

GOD'S PLAN OF RESTORATION IS NEVER JUST FOR YOU

God is the perfect teacher. He uses everything in our lives as an opportunity to teach us valuable life lessons. My prayer life was growing, and it was being used for me in ways far more expansive than just intercession for my husband. God was teaching me lessons I would treasure forever. I probably didn't appreciate them as much back then as I do now because they often came through correction.

Even though I didn't see any lasting changes with Kurt's alcoholism, I always believed that God created Kurt for more than the life he was settling for at the time. My constant prayer was that God would help Kurt become the man of God that he was created to be. One time, I was praying that prayer, and I felt God challenge me. I heard Him softly say to my heart, "Do you want Kurt to be the man I created him to be *for you* or for *Me and My Kingdom*?" Immediately, I felt convicted. God was checking my heart and revealed my true motivation.

> *"All a person's ways seem pure to them,*
> *but motives are weighed by the LORD."*
> PROVERBS 16:2

God always sees beyond the words we speak. He knows the reason we are saying them. On the surface, my prayer seemed genuine, "Please, God, help my husband to be the man you created him to be." Noble words but the true motive of my heart was selfish. God saw behind the scenes. He knew that I was tired of being married to an alcoholic. I was tired of the humiliation of showing up alone to dinner parties with other couples because Kurt was out drinking. I knew that if God helped Kurt overcome his alcoholism, it would definitely benefit *my* life. I was in so much emotional discomfort that the motive of my prayers was to ease my own pain. I confessed, "You're right, God. I admit it. I was praying with selfish motives." God helped me see a bigger picture beyond my own need. God had a purpose and plan for Kurt. The wonderful work of redemption in Kurt's life would reach further than the effect it would have on my marriage. My prayers for Kurt continued on with the new understanding that, although restoration would benefit me, it was for the Kingdom of God.

JUST BEFORE THE BREAKTHROUGH

God is very comforting to us as He works restoration in our lives. However, that doesn't mean that He will not challenge us to take steps of faith and obedience. The longer it took for restoration to happen in my marriage, the more discouraged I became.

It was late at night, Kurt was out, Nicholas was sound asleep, the house was quiet, and I was kneeling at my bedside, crying out to God. This time, the only response I felt from God was, "You are robbing me." I knew what that meant. I heard sermons about tithing, but I didn't tithe. I gave money in the offering, but I didn't tithe. My first response to God was, "Really? Are you kidding me God?" There I was, right on the very edge of despair, pouring my hopeless little heart out to Him, and all He wanted to talk about was *money!* Was this the loving, compassionate, forgiving God I knew? I thought, "How could God be so…so…*insensitive?*" Even though somewhere in my heart I knew God was right, I was too irritated to deal with it. I went to bed quite frustrated. Days passed and my prayer life was pretty much the same every time. I would call out to God, and He would tell me I was robbing Him.

I wish that I could tell you that I humbled myself and just started to tithe, but I didn't. Instead, I decided to negotiate with God. I finally said, "All right, *all right!* Okay, God, I'll make you a deal." I was a sales person working on commission at the time, and I had a really big project I was trying to close. I promised God that I would start tithing if He made a way for me to close this really big deal, and I went to bed that night convinced that I had a deal with Him. I woke up the next morning, went to work, and the phone rang. It was the client with the big project calling to tell me that something had come up, and he had to cancel the project. I hung up the phone, looked up, and asked, "Didn't we have a deal, God?

My prayer life went back to square one; I would pray, and God would say, "You are robbing me," until, one day, I finally surrendered, "Okay, I give up." I made a promise to God that I would tithe on my next commission check no matter how big or small it was. That check was the smallest commission check I've ever received. Now, I wish I could tell you that I gave that first tithe check with a cheerful heart, but I didn't. I gave it with a rotten attitude, mostly because, at the time, I didn't understand what I was learning.

Now, I understand that God really didn't want or need my money. He wanted my complete trust in Him and all His promised blessings.

> *"'Bring the whole tithe into the storehouse,*
> *that there may be food in my house.*
> *Test me in this,' says the LORD Almighty,*
> *'and see if I will not throw open the floodgates*
> *of heaven and pour out so much blessing that there*
> *will not be room enough to store it.'"*
>
> MALACHI 3:10

It was only a few months after I wrote that first tithe check that Kurt checked into a recovery program and received his freedom.

DARKEST BEFORE THE DAWN

Those last few months leading up to the breakthrough I had been praying for were the darkest and ugliest times of our marriage. The night before Kurt went into rehab was an ultimate low for me. I'll be honest with you—I wasn't sure if we would ever have breakthrough or if I was just going to break. I had come to the end of my rope, and I had nothing left. You know that you are on the edge when you lock yourself inside the bathroom, curl up on the floor, and just rock yourself back and forth for hours. That's exactly what I did. It was the night before the Lord would bring the very breakthrough that I had been praying about for years, and I wasn't on my knees praying like usual. I was completely hopeless, locked in my bathroom, and ready to give up. All I kept saying over and over was, "I can't do this anymore…I can't live like this anymore…"

I was so hopeless and weary during those hours that I didn't want to live at all. I couldn't find a reason to get off that bathroom floor. I felt trapped in a broken life and marriage that I couldn't fix. I felt no love in my heart for my husband, my life, or even God. I didn't want to live. My mind thought of ways to end it all. I was in a very spiritually dark moment of my life.

I know that God was right there with me. He was so faithful to me during a time that I was void of faith. He loved me, even when I felt no love for Him.

> *"If we are faithless, he remains faithful,*
> *for he cannot disown himself."*
> 2 TIMOTHY 2:13

> *"We love because he first loved us."*
> 1 JOHN 4:19

As I sat on my bathroom floor rocking myself and feeling completely empty, God helped me to tap into what seemed to be the only love that remained in my heart—a mother's love. God reminded me of my son, Nicholas. It was the love I had for my little boy that gave me the strength to pull myself off the floor and open the door. I had come to a conclusion. I wanted to live life because I was a mother, and in that, I found a reason to fight. I didn't want my little boy to grow up in a crazy lifestyle caused by alcoholism. What I didn't know at that time was that the mother's love in my heart wasn't only for my son. I later found out that, in that very moment, I was already pregnant with our second child, our daughter.

I sat on the couch and waited for Kurt to come home. It was hours later when he finally came stumbling in. I decided to confront him right away. This was not a wise choice.

I tried to reason with an intoxicated man, and that never goes well. The confrontation got really loud and ugly. It finally ended as he turned away from me to pass out on the bed.

I was devastated by the situation. It was an all-time low. The process of restoration is never a pretty road. At times, it can get very dark and ugly. When God is the one guiding you to restoration, He never leaves your side. God is not intimated by the ugliness of our circumstances. He understands that, often-times, it is the very darkest just before the dawn of restoration.

I threw myself at the mercy of God for help. I needed his help for the strength and courage to take the next step. While Kurt was sleeping, I made arrangements with a thir-ty-day recovery program, packed his bags, and waited for him to wake up. When he woke up, we sincerely apologized to each other. Then, I gave him an ultimatum. I told him that I had packed his bags, and he was going to use them one way or the other. He could use them to check himself in and get help at the recovery program. If he was willing to do that, I told him I was willing to walk with him through recovery; if he didn't do that, I told him that he would use the bags I packed to leave my life, our marriage, and our family.

Kurt chose the recovery program. Within that one choice, he chose so much more than just sobriety. He made a choice for God, himself, our family, and me over his addiction. That was August 1990, over twenty years ago. It all came down to a choice that Kurt had to make. God's blessings and my prayers played an important role, but restoration hinged on a choice that my husband made. I am so thankful that Kurt had the courage to face his addiction and the faith to overcome.

God's forgiveness and restoration were evident in Kurt's life from that point forward. Kurt became a completely different person and a truly amazing man of God, far surpassing my prayers for him.

RESTORATION LEADS TO
MORE FORGIVENESS AND HEALING

I thought that Kurt's sobriety would immediately renew our marriage. Instead, I found my mind was filled with questions that I never thought would matter to me. "Where was my husband all those nights he was out getting drunk, and who was he with?" I was secretly holding bitterness against him. I wanted to be free from all the resentment, but the daunting questions raced through my mind, so I talked to Kurt. He patiently answered every one of my questions with integrity, honesty, and humility. His answers were not easy to hear. They confirmed some of my worst fears. It was all out. Everything was on the table: where he had been all those nights, whom he was with, and what he was doing. He cheated, not just once but several times.

I was devastated and felt betrayed. Yet, I knew that the man I was married to was no longer the man who had done these things. God had changed Kurt's heart and life. Now, it was my turn to make a choice. If our marriage was going to have a chance, I would have to choose to partner with God, forgive Kurt for his past betrayals, and let God heal our marriage. As I mentioned in the last chapter, forgiveness was a process of healing for me, one that brought me spiritual freedom and was necessary for the life of our marriage. Forgiveness released our marriage from the ties to the past, giving way to God's beautiful plans for our future. The Bible defines marriage as two becoming one, two individuals willingly making decisions for the unity of one. It takes both parties. Both must make choices placed before them to make the marriage work.

FRUIT OF RESTORATION

About a year into Kurt's sobriety, it was our wedding anniversary. Kurt was out all day taking college classes, and I was home with our son, Nic, and our new baby girl, Katie. I was preparing a steak dinner to celebrate our anniversary, thinking about our marriage and all we had been through. "If anyone deserves a nice anniversary, it's us," I thought to myself. The time for Kurt to return home came and passed. First, he was fifteen minutes late, then thirty minutes, then an hour. With every tick of the clock, anxiety began to well up in my heart. It felt just like before. Painful memories of sleepless nights flooded my mind. Then, the door opened, and Kurt came bouncing in, overflowing with joy. All I could say was, "You're late."

Kurt could hardly contain his excitement. He answered, "I know, I know. Babe, please listen. I met this guy at school today. He is really hurting right now. He needs Jesus. I feel like I am supposed to take him to dinner tonight." I was stunned. I thought for a minute, "Did I just hear that right? Is my husband asking me if he can take some guy he just met out to dinner on our anniversary?" I said, "But it's our anniversary." Kurt quickly responded, "I know, but we will have lots of those. I really need to take him to dinner tonight." Still in shock, I just said, "Okay." With that, he bounced out of the house just as happy as he bounced in. I was not so happy.

I sat down to eat my cold anniversary dinner alone with my children. God gently reminded me of one of the lessons

He taught me. He had challenged the motives of my prayers once: "Do you want Kurt to be a man of God for you or for me?" God had done an amazing work in my husband's life. This miracle was not only for me, our marriage, and our family but for God and His kingdom. The man that Kurt took to dinner that night on our anniversary was the first person Kurt led to Christ. To this day, decades later, Kurt stays in touch with him.

As far as anniversaries go, Kurt was right; we've had lots of those. We have built a life together, raised our children to adulthood together, become grandparents together, and found the priceless gift of lifelong partnership. Every step of the way, no matter how dark our road becomes, God walks with us, lighting the path. His restoration is so much more beautiful than words can express.

CHAPTER 3

Truth

"...He has given us His very great
and precious promises, so that through them
you may participate in the divine nature..."

2 PETER 1:4

Over the years of teaching Bible studies, many people have shared with me their desire to read the Bible and their frustration with it as well. *How* do you read the Bible? I have been asked this question many times. No matter how we choose to read or study it, the Word of God is always life-giving, challenging, and inspiring. I have developed a true love to learn God's promises and share His hope with others, but to be completely honest with you, my devotional time in God's Word has not always been that passionate.

TRUE CONFESSIONS

When I first gave my life to God, I could not get enough of the Bible. Hungry to learn more, I would read for hours and hours. As years passed, my personal Bible reading became less. At one point many years ago when I had two small children, feeling overwhelmed with my "busy" life, I completely stopped reading the Bible on my own. I went to church every Wednesday and Sunday. I would dust off my Bible to follow the pastor's sermon, and then, there my Bible would sit, under the front seat of my car until the next church service.

I made the mistake of placing the burden of my entire spiritual growth upon my pastor. I justified my behavior by telling myself, "You're a busy, young mother; you don't have the time to read the Bible. You are involved with your church, and you are getting good teaching there. " My efforts to ease the ongoing conviction I felt didn't work. I *did* have time for God. I knew I did. I just didn't make the time. Why? Why wasn't I willing to make time for God? I've thought a lot about this, and I think the real reason was because I got comfortable. I got comfortable living a church-going lifestyle. I had been living the Christian life and attending the same church every week for years. I got comfortable. The next thing I knew, it had been months since I had read the Bible on my own without being led by a pastor. My personal relationship with God was suffering, and I was beginning to wonder, "Is this all there is?" The answer, of course, is NO! That's not all there is. God has so much more for us than a mediocre, unfulfilled life.

One beautiful Sunday morning, God captured my heart again. I don't really remember much about the sermon, except that it was about the power of confession, but I will never forget the altar call. The pastor had his leadership team stand up in front and face the congregation. Then, he said something like, "There are many things that can keep us from a close relationship with God, but the power of confession can help make it right. If you would like to come forward to confess, we will pray for you." I struggled with the decision to go forward for a few minutes, wondering what others might think of me. At that time, we attended a very small church, and everyone knew everyone. Yet, my soul longed for the intimate relationship I once had with God.

Then, I caught the eye of the pastor's wife. We were friends, and I felt safe with her. We both had small children at that time, and I thought, "Surely, she'll understand how busy my life is," so I went forward. I tried to make it sound better by saying, "I've been so busy with the kids, and life has been so hectic." Then, I just came out with it, "It's been months since I have read the Bible on my own." Her response was not the one I expected at all, but it was the one I needed. She looked me straight in the eyes and said, "Danise, let's not mince words here. You have been *slothful* in your devotion to God; let's pray against sloth." With that, she took my hands, bowed her head, and prayed for me.

I'll be honest with you, I don't remember any of her prayer. The word "*slothful*" just kept ringing in my head. At first, I was offended by this response. I wasn't a lazy person! Then, I realized that she was right. Although I was diligent in other areas of my life, I had become lazy, and yes, "*slothful*," in my personal time with God. To this day, I am so very thankful that she had the courage to just tell the truth. The truth is not always easy to hear, but the truth always sets us free.

I admitted to God that I had been lazy in my personal devotion with Him and asked for His forgiveness. Immediately, I felt released from the guilt I had been carrying around. At that point, I understood that I had used busyness as an excuse for my laziness with God. That began a new season of spiritual wholeness in my life. Because of that experience, I understand that it is not the responsibility of pastors and speakers to fill us up spiritually—it is our responsibility. Our pastors' words are not intended to be everything we need from God for the entire week. It's unfair to place that unrealistic expectation on them. When we take ownership of our own spiritual growth, we come to church services filled by God and ready to serve, not to be served. If we come to church already spiritually full, we will welcome all the words of life that can be added to us through our pastors.

> *"Jesus answered, 'Everyone who drinks this water*
> *will be thirsty again, but whoever drinks the water*
> *I give them will never thirst. Indeed, the water*
> *I give them will become in them a spring of water*
> *welling up to eternal life.'"*
> JOHN 4:13–14

God desires for us to have a spring of life overflowing from within us that we have been maintaining with Him daily. This can only come by spending intentional time seeking God and His Word for personal purpose. I know that, on the surface, this can sound very self-serving, but it's really not selfish at all. God sees you personally. His heart is for you, and the plans He has for you are to bring you hope and fulfillment. God desires to fill our lives and make us spiritually whole with an overflow of blessings so that we will have plenty to share with others. Longing to fill spiritual emptiness is a universal human need. It begs to be truly satisfied. We can see it all around us and not just in others but within ourselves.

Once, I stood in front of my Bible study class and asked this question, "Do you *need* God every day?" The response was unanimously, "*Yes!*" I believe that within the heart of every person, no matter how deep down it is, there is the realization of a personal, daily need for God. How about you? Do you believe that you *need* God every day? Are you facing obstacles in your life that are bigger than your ability to handle them? Is life challenging you with situations that need God's direction? Realizing our need for God is actually the key to enjoying life-changing devotions with God every day. If we believe that we need God daily and we desire to unlock the power of this revelation, then we have to ask God *how* we need Him every day.

We all seem to have the basic understanding that we need God, but if we are being honest with ourselves, are we really taking the time to acknowledge that need to *Him* every day? Do we ask Him to show us how we need Him? When we are completely vulnerable with God, we begin to understand ourselves in new ways, and through His great promises, we discover the full life we were always meant to have.

The following five steps can transform Bible reading into life-changing steps to spiritual fulfillment every day.

FIVE STEPS TO FILL OUR NEEDS WITH GOD'S TRUTH

1. Identify our needs

2. Fill our needs with God's truth

3. Believe the truth

4. Apply the truth

5. Share the truth

Identify our needs

*"[Y]our father knows
what you need before you ask Him."*

MATTHEW 6:8

Not only does God know our needs before we do, He also knows exactly how to fill those needs. He knows what we need even better than we do. He knows all our life situations, our innermost thoughts, and He sees to the deepest part of our heart and soul. Those places no one else can see are in the Lord's clear view. We are completely known by Him. No facades or screens can hide the reality of who we are and what we really need from God's sight. Such vulnerability might feel uncomfortable, but it is the most impacting way to begin our time in God's Word. David penned my favorite prayer in the entire Bible. He lays his heart out before God with no barriers as he welcomes the Lord to search his heart and mind with complete trust.

> *"Search me, God, and know my heart;*
> *test me and know my anxious thoughts.*
> *See if there is any offensive way in me*
> *and lead me in the way everlasting."*
>
> PSALM 139:23–24

It isn't until after David invites God to see and know everything, and to test everything within him, that he then asks God to lead him. If we continually ask God to lead us without first laying ourselves humbly exposed before Him, we miss a very important step.

Complete vulnerability means nothing is off limits; there are no walls. It's letting God into every area of our mind, heart, and behavior. God is our only constant safe place. He is our hiding place where vulnerability is no longer scary. He knows everything, and He sees everything, and yet, He unconditionally loves us. He understands us better than we even understand ourselves. Vulnerability with God can start with a simple little prayer from the heart: "God please shine the light of your presence into every area of my life." If we invite God to shine His holy light into every area of our life, our needs and voids will definitely be revealed. No one can stand in the presence of a holy God without something being uncovered. The condition of our mind, the burdens of the heart, and the motives of our behavior are exposed. In these precious moments with God, don't hold anything back. Don't try to cover up things that are embarrassing, shameful, and sinful. God never uncovers with the intention of harming us. His purpose is always to restore, heal, and fill us to overflowing with His hope.

Psalm 145:18 tells us, "The Lord is near to all who call on Him." We can seek God with confidence, knowing that He will respond to us when we call on Him. I think it's safe to say that we all have a general knowledge of what's going on in our own lives. Because of that, we also have a pretty good idea of our personal needs. Beginning our Bible time in vulnerable prayer allows God to help us more clearly define those needs. God is the one who knows us and our needs better than we do.

Fill our needs with God's truth

"And God is able to bless you abundantly,
so that in all things at all times, having all that
you need, you will abound in every good work."

2 Corinthians 9:8

"The Lord will guide you always.
He will satisfy your needs."

Isaiah 58:11

"My God will meet all your needs according to His
glorious riches in Christ Jesus."

Philippians 4:19

In this step, we find promises in the Word of God that specifically address our needs. God's scriptures are relevant to our individual lives today. We can discover this in a personal way by using a simple tool, such as a concordance, to look up Bible verses and stories that fit our specific need. I'll use myself as an example; let's say I have been struggling with a bad attitude, and I am in need of an attitude adjustment. This actually happens more often than I would like to admit. Bible verses on topics such as humility, kindness, patience, and love speak right to the heart of my need. This requires some intentional searching, but it's surprising how quickly we can create a personalized Bible study that perfectly fits our need. It's possible to have a meaningful and life-changing devotional time every day.

Every time we let God comfort or challenge us personally with His Word, our faith in God becomes more real in our lives. It is when we rely on our own strength that we are in danger of being deceived.

> *"[Y]ou have eaten the fruit of deception*
> *because you have depended on your own strength."*
> HOSEA 10:13

The more dependent we are on God, the more rooted in truth we become.

When we read the Bible with personal purpose, we uncover the truth that can truly satisfy our soul. Filling our needs with His divine Word is literally only minutes away. God doesn't need hours to minister to us. I am often amazed at how much God is able to accomplish in my heart and mind within the first five minutes of reading the Bible with personal purpose. God can work fast, but once we have experienced a truly personalized devotional time, we long for more.

Believe the truth

*"Then Jesus said, 'Did I not tell you
that if you believe, you will see the glory of God?'"*

John 11:40

We often hear the saying, "You can't always believe what you read." When reading the Bible, it is the exact opposite; *always* believe what you read. Years ago, while attending a women's conference, the speaker said something that made an impact on my life and has stayed with me ever since. She said, "The problem with Christians is that we *know* what we *believe*; we just don't really *believe* what we *know*." I remember thinking, "That's it!" It is such a simple statement and yet so powerful and true. I was compelled to ask myself a question, "Do I really believe what I know from the Bible?" If we really want to receive and accomplish all that God has for us, it's going to take more than just reading and knowing the Bible. We have to believe what the Bible tells us. Jesus says that if we believe, we will see the glory of God. If we want to see the glory of God in our lives and share His glory with others, we need faith to believe what we read in the Bible.

Bible promises can fulfill our lives and make us spiritually whole. However, the power found in God's Word can only be released into our lives when we really believe in its promises. Until then, God's promises sit like unopened gifts. A Bible scripture can be the source of hope, joy, and spiritual freedom to one who believes. Yet, to those who don't believe what they read, it is nothing more than a sentence on a page. The difference between experiencing the life that God has planned for us and forfeiting those plans is faith. Faith helps us to open all the gifts that God has for our lives. What glorious gifts does

God have prepared for each of us? When we have faith in the promises of God, He begins to reveal in very personal and powerful ways how relevant His promises are to us.

Believe what you read in the Bible, and invite the glory of God into your life every day. Don't you wish it was as easy to do this as it is to say it? I do. Of course, it's not that easy. The first challenge I faced was that I found it easier to believe God's promises for someone else than for myself. Sometimes the situations in our lives do not seem to measure up to the promises we find in God's Word.

The facts are not always the truth. Often we allow our circumstances to dictate our faith. It should be the opposite; our faith should dictate our circumstances. We aren't alone in our weakness. Throughout the Bible, there are stories of mighty men and women of faith who were faced with the same battle we are. It's the battle of *truth* versus *fact*. We face this battle any time we want to step out in faith, and the facts in our lives seem to contradict the promises we read in the Bible. Peter faced the battle of Truth versus Fact when Jesus called him to step out of the boat and walk to Him on the water.

Peter was surrounded by the *facts* of his situation. The waves crashing all around him were the *facts*. Jesus, who was walking on top of the waves and clearly not affected at all by the *facts* of Peter's situation, extended His hand to Peter and said, "Come." Peter stepped out of the boat onto real waves. The *facts* in Peter's situation were real; they were real waves and could drown him, but the *faith* he had in God was *truth*. Facts might be real, but our faith is not found in the facts—faith is always found in the truth. As Peter kept his eyes focused on Jesus and his promise (the truth), he walked over the waves (the facts) as though they weren't there at all.

Our faith in God's truth can prevail over our *facts* when we, like Peter, keep our eyes on God and His promises. Although *facts* are real, they aren't always the *truth*. Yes, it's true that Peter took his eyes off of Jesus, and as he looked at the waves (the facts) instead of Jesus (the truth), he began to sink. However, he didn't drown. Jesus rescued him in the midst of his doubt. It might have only been for a short time, but Peter still walked over those waves like they weren't even there. So what if he got a little wet at the end? He stepped out in faith and saw the glory of God at work in his life. He also discovered that, even when his faith failed him, God never did. God is always faithful. The facts in our lives are never bigger than the truth of God's promises. The challenge to our faith will always be to believe the truth that we read in the Bible, in spite of the facts of our circumstances. It is then that we begin to see the glory of God at work in our lives!

Belief equals faith. We can strengthen our faith by training ourselves to believe. Faith comes from hearing.

> *"Consequently, faith comes from hearing the message, and the message is heard through the word about Christ."*
>
> ROMANS 10:17

We can increase our faith in God's Word every day by simply speaking Bible scriptures out loud that address our personal needs. Notice I said speak the scriptures out loud, not just read them. What's the difference? Faith. Speak the scriptures out loud in faith and believe that those are personal promises and God's blessings over your life. Everyday, you will be hearing a personal Bible study designed just for you and training yourself in faith in the process.

Apply the truth

"Therefore, everyone who hears these words of mine
and puts them into practice
is like a wise man who built his house on the rock."

MATTHEW 7:24

We all desire to be like the wise man Jesus describes in this scripture. However, the only way to turn knowledge into wisdom is to put knowledge into practice. Once we have partnered with God to read and believe the promises in the Bible, our daily partnership with Him continues as we learn to apply what we have learned in our life. Putting our belief into practice brings the promises of God to life. Just as faith is required to believe, life application requires surrender to God's way. Surrendering our will to God's will is our opportunity to crown God the Lord over our personal lives. Whether we have walked with God for seventy years or seven days, it is a daily choice to lay aside our way in order to take up God's way for our lives. It is important for us to remember that God's ways are *not* our ways.

"'For my thoughts are not your thoughts,
neither are your ways my ways,' declares the Lord."

ISAIAH 55:8

On the one hand, this scripture is encouragement to us. It is comforting to know that God's promises are large enough to fill the voids we have in life because His ways are higher than ours. However, this scripture is also a challenge. To put God's ways into practice, we must be willing to say yes to God's instruction, and that often means saying no to our way of doing things. God understands how difficult this is for us, and He has equipped us for this challenge.

*"And you also were included in Christ when you
heard the word of truth, the gospel of your salvation:
Having believed you were marked in Him with
a seal, the promised Holy Spirit; who is a deposit
guaranteeing our inheritance..."*

EPHESIANS 1:13–14

The day we heard the truth of God's plan for salvation and we believed that truth, God did something incredible. He sealed His promise to us with the Holy Spirit. God made an investment in us. God deposited His very own Spirit within us as His personal guarantee to us that all God's promises are fulfilled through our new inheritance in Christ. Romans 8:26 tells us, "The Spirit helps us in our weakness." As we feel the struggle between surrendering to God's will or our own, the Holy Spirit is always strong enough to help us apply the truth to live for Him.

Share the truth

*"(God) comforts us in all our troubles,
so that we can comfort those in any trouble
with the comfort we ourselves receive from God."*

2 CORINTHIANS 1:4

When we let God change, one day at a time, our personal world behind closed doors, we are equipped to step out and be world changers one person at a time. Personal fulfillment is only the beginning benefit of believing and applying God's promises in our lives. We are not truly satisfied and complete until we share what we have been given with others. Sharing what we have makes it worth having. His spiritual blessings in our lives were never intended for us to hoard. There is a spiritual fullness that can only be acquired when we see the fruit of our personal devotional time not only alive in our own lives, but actually helpful to someone else. The purpose of spiritual fulfillment is not exclusively for our personal benefit but to bring healing and hope to others as well.

In essence, this is my true reason for writing this book. Each day, *I* am personally in need of God. Each day, He leads me with His comfort and guidance. I have been discouraged, and God has given me hope. I've experienced lack, and God has provided. I have worried, and God has given me peace. I have allowed bitterness to burrow its way into my heart, and God has shown me the way to forgiveness. I was spiritually blind, but everyday, God helps me see. He continues to be my divine mentor, teaching and leading me through all the seasons of my life. God fulfills my life with His truth, and then, as I share this hope He has given to me, His truth brings freedom to others.

There are no greater spiritual gems to be found than the pearls of life we personally discover during our own time with God. Every day, His comfort and guidance are waiting for us to find in His Word. As God daily meets our needs through His amazing promises, we are encouraged to share that hope with someone else.

CHAPTER 4

Breaking Free

*"Then, you will know the truth,
and the truth will set you free."*

JOHN 8:32

The preacher stands up and declares these encouraging words, "Your past does not define your future." The sound of claps and cheers can be heard as these life-giving words ring true in the hearts of those in the church. We all deeply desire to believe that we are not bound by the mistakes of our past or limited by the success of yesterday. It isn't just an inspirational saying. It is a promise from God: we will know the truth, and His truth will set us free.

*"Therefore, if anyone is in Christ, the new creation
has come: The old has gone, the new is here!"*

2 CORINTHIANS 5:17

Have you ever been frustrated because you want to believe that you are a new creation in Christ, but sometimes, you feel like your life is a runaway train, and you are a passenger doomed to sit helplessly as you watch yourself make the same mistakes over and over again? I have. It's because the old mentalities, the behaviors of our past, and our sin nature are battling the God-given spirit of freedom within us.

What is spiritual freedom, and how do we attain it? The answers to those questions are best outlined in the following scripture.

"[L]et us throw off everything that hinders
and the sin that so easily entangles, and let us run
with perseverance the race marked out for us.
Let us fix our eyes on Jesus."
HEBREWS 12:1–2

There is a common desire among us all to fulfill our true purpose—"the race marked out for us." There is a potential within each of us that God himself has designed uniquely for us. Our soul longs to discover and complete all that our divine creator has placed inside of us. As we run our race, we will encounter obstacles that can only be overcome by aligning ourselves with God's way, not our own. We need to identify and "throw off everything that hinders" us from becoming and doing all that God has planned for us. To "throw off" is to free ourselves from a burden. "Everything" means anything that is keeping us from reaching our full potential in Christ. This scripture tells us that there are two different types of things we are to throw off: hindrances and sin. Hindrances can sometimes be sinful, but sometimes, they are burdens we needlessly carry. God leads us to freedom one thought at a time. Old ways of thinking that don't measure up to God's truth can hold us back from believing God's promises or reaching our full potential in Christ.

Roller Coasters

I am a huge fan of roller coasters. That might even be an understatement. I enjoy roller coasters so much that I actually broke an amusement park record when I rode the same coaster one hundred and fifty times in one day. I have a season pass to an amusement park that is known for its extreme rides. One of my favorite things to do is drive to the park on a lunch break just to ride one roller coaster.

I love the adrenaline rush as I twist and turn, hands up, smiling, and laughing through all the ups and downs. There is something to be said about living our lives with that kind of surrender to God through all the unpredictable twists of life. It's a priceless gift to discover a faith that is so strong that we can enjoy life no matter the ups and downs we face.

There is a lifestyle roller coaster that I rode for many years. It's one that I built with my own hands, crafted over years of mental conditioning—the roller coaster of people pleasing. I never enjoyed that ride, yet I would regularly strap myself into the seat and endure its agonizing ups and downs. I felt lost as my identity would change with the opinions of those around me. I would choose to be up when people were happy with me and then plummet quickly downward at the sign of negativity. Freedom called to me from the truth written in God's Word, "I love you, *always*, unconditionally. Live for Me. Live for an audience of One." The thought of freedom from the insecurity seemed too good to be true. Could it be? Could God reach down that deep inside of me and free me from the only roller coaster I've never liked? Yes.

Jesus stood at the station, waiting for me as I finished the ride. My hands weren't up; my knuckles were white as I tightly clutched the safety bar. There were no smiles or sounds of laughter, only the look of disillusion as I struggled to remember who I was. With one hand extended to me, He motioned with His other to unbuckle the seat belt I had strapped myself with countless times. God was right there; freedom was within my reach. It would have to be my choice. His eyes of love gave me the strength to let go of false security and step into my true identity in Him. Sometimes, the old familiar roller coaster of people pleasing tempts me to ride again. Every time, it's a shorter and shorter ride.

I like people, and I hope people like me, but I'm okay if they don't. You can never please everyone all the time, but freedom has taught me that there is security found in living to please One. Spiritual freedom is a powerful reality that God can teach us to live in every day.

> *"It is for freedom that Christ has set us free.*
> *Stand firm, then and do not let yourselves be*
> *burdened again by a yoke of slavery."*
> GALATIANS 5:1

Freedom is a gift that God freely and lovingly gives to all of His children through Christ Jesus, but it is also very much our daily choice. We have to make the decision whether we will accept and walk in the spiritual fulfillment that Christ gave to us. It is our responsibility and privilege to make the choice to throw off the perspectives that have hindered our lives. Our willingness, combined with the power of God at work within us, will produce a fulfilled life in Christ. Spiritual freedom is like a personalized gift from God, designed to equip and help us in our lives. The gift is all wrapped up and waiting for each of us to open. The question is whether we will choose to do our part to live our lives with the freedom God has given to us. We actually have control of the runaway train or roller coaster that once dictated our lives.

THREE STEPS TO BREAKING FREE

1. **Identify the lies**

2. **Replace the lies with the truth**

3. **Pray for god's help and guidance**

Identify the lies

By "lies," I mean powerful thoughts that have the ability to form what we believe, but when compared to the truth of God's Word, they would be considered false. Initially, it is difficult to identify these thoughts as lies because we have often accepted them as truth for so long. If we have lived with a particular thought pattern for a long time, it actually becomes more comfortable to believe in a lie than to embrace God's truth. The only way we can discern whether a thought is a lie or truth is to measure it against the truth of God's Word.

I spent the first twenty-one years of my life forming many of my own opinions, so when I began to accept God's truth in my life, it was like I was trying to wear a jacket that didn't fit me. I would try to believe God's promises, but at the same time, I would also feel the old mindsets pulling me back. Concerning our past, even when we have worked through forgiveness, sometimes there are still some unhealthy thought patterns left for us to work through. Spiritual hindrances can often be found in lies from our past that were planted in our heart and reinforced through trauma of some kind. Words that we have heard spoken to us and experiences we have lived through can have the ability to form very strong mindsets and influence our perspective. This is why we have to be truly honest and genuinely ask ourselves some questions:

What thoughts or beliefs do I struggle with that keep me from experiencing freedom? Are there events from my past or words that were spoken to me that are making it difficult for me to accept truth of God's Word?

Replace the lies with the truth

Once we have uncovered the lies in our thought patterns, it's time to replace them with the truth. The Bible is filled with scriptures that will set us free from lies we once believed. This is a process and sometimes feels like a losing battle. Day-by-day, thought-by-thought, we begin to retrain our thinking to align with God's promises of freedom instead of the old thoughts that were formed over time and from experiences. When Jesus was in the desert and the devil was trying to tempt Him with lies, Jesus battled the lies with God's truth. This will require either a little knowledge of God's Word or a little effort to find the truth that replaces the lie. We will always discover that there are many more promises of truth than there are lies.

EXAMPLES OF
REPLACING LIES WITH THE TRUTH

The Lie—I'm not loved or accepted.

The Truth—
God lavishes His love on me
and called me His child (1 JOHN 3:1).

The Truth—
God's great love toward me
endures forever (PSALM 117:2).

The Truth—
God's loves me so much that He sent His Son Jesus
to make a way for my freedom (JOHN 3:16, JOHN 8:36).

The Lie—I'm going to fail. I feel like a failure.

The Truth—
God gives me victory in Christ
(1 CORINTHIANS 15:57).

The Truth—
God will finish the good work He started in me
(PHILIPPIANS 1:6).

The Truth—
I can do all things through Christ
who gives me strength
(PHILIPPIANS 4:13).

Pray for God's help and guidance

Freedom is not a product of our power or strength but the power of God's Spirit. We need to partner with God continually through prayer as He guides us to victory. Communication with Him is key; God wants to reveal Himself and His promises to you. Pray for the ability to discern the difference between hindering lies and His truth that sets you free. Pray for His guidance to direct you as you search for His truth and let go of the lies.

FREE TO SERVE

*"You, my brothers and sisters, were called to be free.
But do not use your freedom to indulge the flesh;
rather, serve one another humbly in love."*
GALATIANS 5:13

Freedom has a deeper purpose for us beyond equipping and helping us to reach our God-given potential. It's not to be used for selfish gain or sinful reasons. It is meant to help us better serve one another with the love of Christ. The moment we are willing to surrender to God's way, we are filled with a renewed strength and a lighter burden. Following Christ becomes a lot easier when we aren't toting a heavy backpack of unnecessary baggage with us. The hindrances we allow to control us not only hold us back, but they inhibit our ability to serve others with the love Christ. Choosing spiritual freedom is a gift to our own lives and empowers us to bless others. The process of freedom is genuinely fulfilled when we discover that God's purpose for our freedom reaches far beyond our own personal benefit.

CHAPTER 5

Change

*"...where the Spirit of the Lord is, there is freedom.
We...are being transformed into His image
with ever-increasing glory..."*

2 CORINTHIANS 3:17-18

Once our heart is surrendered to Christ, we enter into the process of change. God has declared that we are free, new, and sanctified in Christ, yet we are all in the process of being transformed into His image every day. I believe in a perfect God who faithfully remains the same from generation to generation. He never changes, but with His careful guidance, we are always changing. God is our creator and desires to mold us into the completely beautiful creation He has planned for us to be. He restrains His power and waits for us to willingly yield to the work of His hands. Once we are pliable with complete trust in Him, all things become possible, and all limitations crumble at the force of His majesty. Unbelievable and even miraculous changes begin to take form as we, His creation, work together in harmony with our creator. God has formed amazing plans that lay just beneath the surface within us, waiting for the moment we are willing to change.

Have you ever felt like you needed some positive change in your life? Have you tried to change but were unsuccessful?

Maybe you tried, not just once or twice, but over and over again. Me too. I've learned that there is a pattern to this cycle. It always begins with that moment when we realize something needs to change. That moment is always followed by good intentions, but no matter how good the intentions are, they don't last. Then, the fall comes, and the old habits creep back in. The cycle starts again and plays on repeat over and over. Every time, it becomes more difficult to believe that true change will ever happen. Genuine change is possible when it starts from the inside and then moves to outward behavior.

I am personally speaking of the decades I struggled with food addiction. Of course, I spent years trying to call it something else. It was an unhealthy diet or lack of exercise or portion control or learning moderation. I called it anything but an addiction. It's true that I needed to change my diet, exercise more, watch portions, and learn moderation, but nothing really changed until I dealt with the core of the issue, my addiction to food. There was a time when I used to turn to food for reward, comfort, guilt, anxiety—even self-punishment. That is what I used to do but not anymore because true change can happen.

Previously, I shared very openly about my husband's addiction to alcohol and the restoration God brought to him and our marriage. On one hand, I walked several difficult years with Kurt through his season of addiction. On the other hand, Kurt walked with me through *decades* of my addiction. He watched me go through the ups and downs. He witnessed all my failed attempts to change. Through it all, he always made me feel loved, desired, and beautiful, even during the times when my five-foot, three-inch body tipped the scales at nearly two hundred pounds. He had a front row seat to all my self-hatred and frustration. A while back, he gave me the most amazing compliment. He said, "You've changed." I lost the weight and kept it off, but he wasn't referencing the changes in my physical body; he meant I had overcome. He was right. I learned how to break the cycle of failure I was in. God helped me to change. While I was on the journey to breaking the cycle, I learned these seven steps to lasting change. Over time, I have shared these steps with many people who desired positive change in their lives. No matter what type of change we seek to make when applying these principles as we partner with God, we will see the lasting change we have been longing for.

Seven Principles of Lasting Change

1. **Revelation:**
   Change needs to happen

2. **Education:**
   Change what we know

3. **Proclamation:**
   Change what we say

4. **Meditation:**
   Change what we think

5. **Action:**
   Change what we do

6. **Motivation:**
   Change takes time, so don't quit

7. **Recognition:**
   Change what we see

Revelation: Change needs to happen

*"Not that I have already obtained all this, or have
already arrived at my goal, but I press on to take
hold of that for which Christ Jesus took hold of me.
Brothers and sisters, I do not consider myself yet to
have taken hold of it. But one thing I do: Forgetting
what is behind and straining toward what is ahead, I
press on toward the goal to win the prize for which
God has called me heavenward in Christ Jesus."*

PHILIPPIANS 3:12–14

Revelation is the moment or the progression of moments when justification stops, we see the truth of what is, and we catch a hopeful glimpse of what could be. Sometimes, we encounter revelation for change through a single encounter with God. Other times, revelation is a long process as God patiently reveals the need for change slowly over time. The relationships in our lives tend to become a mirror, reflecting back to us the image of our true self. God often uses the close relationships in our lives to press in and bring to the surface the areas of our lives in need of change.

Truth ultimately brings freedom. However, because the truth is uncompromising by nature, it can also initially bring some temporary pain. It is not easy to look at one's self without the facade of justification. We have to be willing to honestly look at ourselves for exactly who we are and where we are. We must take it in and love ourselves with the grace of God in spite of our desperate need for change.

For many years, I remained stuck in my food addiction because I found it so hard to love myself through revelation. I had the conviction that I needed to change over and over again.

I became so disappointed in myself that I wasn't able to accept grace, and consequently, I stagnated in my addiction. I felt like I was doomed to stay in the never-ending cycle of desiring change but never actually accomplishing it.

A complete revelation will not happen if we only concentrate on the reality of what currently exist. We must also embrace the possibility of what could be discovered through change. Revelation must give way to resolve. In order to move from revelation to the resolution for change, we have to shift from conviction to hope. Conviction that refuses to become hope will give way to shame, guilt, and condemnation. Hope prepares us to take the next steps into our new future.

Education: Change what we know

*"Call to me, and I will answer you and tell you
great and unsearchable things you do not know."*
JEREMIAH 33:3

Education is learning something new. If we want to change, we have to be willing and humble enough to be teachable. Humility is the ability to admit that whatever we have done before didn't work, at least not long term. Therefore, we need to cultivate a passion for learning new things in the area of our life that needs to change. This step in the process of change requires a heart within us that cries out, "Teach me something new, Lord." When we search to learn more about the changes we need to make, we will find that God will give us valuable advice from many different sources. The foundation of this education process is the wisdom and truth of the Bible, and the building blocks for change can be found from many other sources, such as mentors, professionals, books, websites, podcasts, and even music. Infusing our lives with both biblical and practical tools is necessary for complete change to take place.

With God's truth continually at the core of my journey to overcome food addiction, I also educated myself about kinesiology, nutrition, exercise, breaking thought patterns, and goal setting. God used countless resources, including many educated people, to equip me for the breakthrough I desired. This doesn't have to be an expensive process. Do you know someone who you really admire in the area that you feel you need to change? Why not invite that person to lunch, explaining your desire to learn and asking for any advice he or she would be willing to share? The desire to learn must be bigger than the fear we have to step out and learn something new. Engaging in this step of change to expand our knowledge is quite an adventure all on its own.

Proclamation: Change what we say

"The tongue has the power of life and death,
and those who love it will eat its fruit."
PROVERBS 18:21

"Or take ships as an example. Although they are so
large and are driven by strong winds, they are steered
by a very small rudder wherever the pilot wants to go.
Likewise, the tongue is a small part of the body, but it
makes great boasts. Consider what a great forest is set
on fire by a small spark."
JAMES 3:4-5

The words we speak set the tone of our attitudes and our environment. Like a small rudder directs the course of a huge ship, our tongue is powerful enough to set in motion a brand new course for our lives, either good or bad. Choosing to be intentional with our words is the same as intentionally choosing the direction our path will take. Likewise, allowing our words to simply follow the comfort of habit or emotions will also guide us down a path. Unfortunately, this route is usually the one that circles the same old bush we have gone around a hundred times with no vision or destination in sight. Whether they are filled with meaning and purpose or they are careless, our words set a path. I have seen the benefits and the consequences of this truth play out in my life many times.

When I was around three years old, I had an accident on a playground. I walked between the swings and was hit full force in the mouth by another child swinging. The impact of the swing tore the side of my lip and cut halfway through my tongue. The injury to my tongue was so bad that it took over a year to heal. My mom had to re-teach me to form words and speak again. I nearly lost my tongue, and I often think about what an amazing gift it is just to be able to talk.

Sometimes, I feel like I am using my tongue as the true gift it was intended to be, like when I am praying; singing worship to God; or speaking words of encouragement, love, faith, direction, and hope. But then, there are the times, more often than I would like to admit, when I squander God's gracious gift to me. With my words, I have torn myself down and wounded others. It's in those times that I am the most in awe of God's grace. He knew all the words I would speak with my tongue, the good ones and the horrible ones. In spite of the fact that I have proven to be so inconsistent with my words, He still spared my tongue and, with it, gave me the power of life and death. I admit that I have always found it easier to verbally encourage others than myself. Especially regarding body image, my words were harsh and unforgiving. When I referred to myself, I used words that I wouldn't use to describe someone else. Learning to speak words of affirmation for myself was a challenge for me. I remember starting the process by saying out loud, "I receive the grace of God." Before I left for the gym in the morning, I would literally put my hands on the top of my head and say, "Thank you, God, that you cover me with your grace from the top of my head to the tips of my toes!" Slowly, those simple words of grace began to reform the bleak opinion I once had of myself, and I began to develop a more positive outlook.

We're all fallible and guilty of misusing our words. Yet, God chooses to empower each of us anyway. It is God's intention that our words make a difference. We have been given the privilege to decide what kind of difference they will make. If we desire to see lasting change in our lives, it will always be accompanied by a positive change in the words that come out of our mouth. We will begin to notice a renewal in our speech as we train ourselves to align our words with the new things God is teaching us.

Meditation: Change what we think

"We demolish arguments and every pretension that sets itself up against the knowledge of God, and we take captive every thought to make it obedient to Christ."

2 CORINTHIANS 10:5

As we walk through these steps and begin to learn and speak new things, we soon discover that these new concepts are challenging to our current thought process. Changing what we think goes hand-in-hand with changing what we say. Throughout the day, our minds are filled with thoughts. Some of those thoughts are intentional, and others are nothing more than habit. When trying to break our bad habits, it is important to remember that the behavior we are attempting to change is found in our thoughts as well. We have the ability and power to take captive every thought, especially our own. Paying close attention to the things we are thinking about is a very intentional choice. Next, we recognize any stagnate thoughts that would keep us from moving forward in a positive way and replace them with a mindset that will encourage the changes we are attempting to make.

During my health and fitness journey, I had a wonderful physical trainer who would always call me an athlete. The first time he said that, I just rolled my eyes and laughed because I never would have referred to myself that way. He quickly corrected me and told me that he was referring to the hidden athlete inside of me, who I was training to become. I began to consider myself as an athlete in training. Although, at the time, it seemed to be a big stretch from the truth, changing my thought process in that small way helped me make the changes I desired.

Training our mind to refocus isn't an easy task. It is accomplished over time with many small, calculated decisions to determine the path we want our thoughts to take. There are things that happen in life that are out of our control; however, the things we are thinking and saying are completely under our authority. Accepting this responsibility and taking ownership of our minds is a big step to successful, lasting change.

Action: Change what we do

"No discipline seems pleasant at the time, but painful.
Later on, however, it produces a harvest of righteousness
and peace for those who have been trained by it."

HEBREWS 12:11

Although the previous steps play a vital role in making needed changes, it's not going to be enough to learn about change, talk about change, and think about change. The changes we desire will never come to fruition unless we actually make the effort to do what is needed. We have to be willing to train ourselves to do things differently than we have before. As we begin to make changes in our lives, we become increasingly aware of our need for God's grace to help us put them into practice. The Bible says that self-discipline is a fruit of the Holy Spirit. As with any other training process, self-discipline never seems very pleasant at the time. It's uncomfortable to apply the new things we have learned, but God promises that training in discipline will produce a harvest of good things.

I believe that we are capable of doing a lot more than we think we can. If we are willing to be stretched beyond our limited view, God will lead us to places and equip us to do things we never thought we could do. A few years ago, I felt the Lord challenge me with a theme for the year. The word He gave me was self-discipline. There were two specific areas God wanted me to focus on: my prayer life and fitness.

The Lord had me begin three daily prayer journals, each of them for a special purpose. Every day, I wrote out a prayer in each of those journals. When I started, I wasn't sure I would make it all the way through the first year, consistently writing in those journals. But, I did. Every year, God has been adding to it. Now, I write in six different prayer journals daily. I never would have believed that I'd have the time to do that. If we are willing to be trained in self-discipline, God will help us plan our time.

I found out that my body was able to do a lot more than I thought it could when I joined a fitness challenge. Working out six days a week, sometimes two workouts a day, and following a strict nutrition plan took an enormous amount of self-discipline. That process went from difficult to painful and then turned into an incredible benefit to my overall health. I lost weight and reached goals I once thought were impossible, but I also gained new healthy patterns that have set new fitness standards for my life. If we are willing to be trained in self-discipline, God will exceed our expectations and help us achieve lasting change.

Motivation: Change takes time, so don't quit

"Let us not become weary in doing good,
for at the proper time we will reap a harvest
if we do not give up."

GALATIANS 6:9

"Yet this I call to mind and therefore I have hope:
Because of the Lord's great love we are not consumed,
for his compassions never fail. They are new every
morning; great is your faithfulness."

LAMENTATIONS 3:21–23

The process of changing behavior is very difficult. While we are in the training process, there are bound to be temporary fallbacks into the old patterns. When these discouraging moments come our way, it is important to be prepared to handle them well. We have to fight the tendency to quit. It's interesting how quickly we are willing to give up on ourselves, but we often have patience to endure with hope for others.

Have you ever helped potty train a toddler? It's a messy experience. There are many accidents along the way, but ultimately, the training succeeds. Would any of us tell a little toddler to quit potty training after a few accidents? No, of course we wouldn't. But, that's exactly how we respond to ourselves when our training process gets a little messy. God desires to teach us grace. We receive it new and fresh daily from Him. We must learn to extend that same grace and patience to ourselves just long enough to hang in there and keep going.

Training is hard work, and it can make us tired. Sometimes we just want a break from the training. If we really need a break, we should take one. Remember that a break is a predetermined amount of time. We should decide exactly how much "bench time" we are allowing ourselves and then get up and get back in the game. Powerful, even life-changing results can happen by simply making the firm decision to keep going. Temporary discouragement should never become a reason to continue living with an unhealthy pattern. Don't quit.

Recognition: Change what we see

"'For I know the plans I have for you,' declares the Lord, 'plans to prosper you and not to harm you, plans to give you hope and a future.'"
JEREMIAH 29:11

God not only knows the good plans He has for us, but He sees them coming to full fruition. The final change is to let go of the image we have of ourselves based on our past. We must change the way we view ourselves to reflect the future changes being made in our lives. It won't matter how much behavior we are able to successfully change if we continue to see ourselves as the same people we were before.

There were times throughout my fitness journey that, although my behavior changed and my body reflected those positive results, I still saw myself as the two-hundred-pound version. In the very beginning of my transformation process, I went to my first spin class. I was completely out of shape and felt extremely insecure. It didn't help that the aisles were very narrow between the bikes, and considering the size of my body at the time, I required a little more personal space. As I tried to maneuver my way around, my rear side accidently bumped into the woman next to me. I turned to apologize to her, but she just glared at me with annoyance as if to say, "Clearly you don't belong here."

Over time, my body got a lot smaller, but I still saw myself as the awkward woman in the gym who didn't belong. I didn't even realize that I was doing this until I was talking with a friend much later. She was telling me about another one of her friends who had just started coming to the gym. She showed up to a morning exercise class but decided to turn around and walk out when she saw that all the women there were already in shape. I spoke up right away and said, "But, wait, that's the class I go to; she must have been encouraged when she saw me." My friend just gave me a puzzled look and said, "Danise, you're fit." A light bulb went off over my head as I realized that I was so busy focusing on the process of change that I never took time to acknowledge all the progress I made. Little by little, one baby step at a time, I was changing, inside and out.

We must be willing to free ourselves from old self-images and unrealistic expectations. Throughout the process of change, it is important to take time to celebrate the baby steps and begin to recognize our new selves.

CHAPTER 6

Identity

"...so in Christ all will be made alive."

1 CORINTHIANS 15:22

Simply stated, identity is the condition of being oneself. A fundamental part of living a fulfilled life is knowing and understanding who we are. Once the wisdom of true identity settles its roots in our heart, we're equipped to walk throughout the seasons of life with a steadfast stability.

THE IMPORTANCE OF FAMILY

So often our identity is discovered through our experience of family. Perspectives of family differ from one person to the next. My definition of family changed drastically when I was nine years old. Up to that point, my understanding of family included my parents; my brother; my grandmother; and a few aunts, uncles, and cousins. Then, one day, my mom divorced my dad to be with another man. My dad moved out, and my mom moved my brother and me in with this new man in her life. Instantly, my world changed and so did everything I ever believed about family.

Before the divorce, we moved a lot. I think we moved about seven times by the time I was nine years old. That caused some insecurity and instability in my life. Up to that point, my parents seemed to be the only consistent things anchoring me. Their separation created an even greater sense of uncertainty within me. Our experience and concept of family impacts our identity deeply.

Soon after the divorce, I had stepparents; step-grandparents; stepbrothers; stepaunts, uncles, and cousins. People I had never met became my "family." The adjustment was difficult, mostly because I wasn't sure of where I belonged. As I maneuvered through this new lifestyle, there were some benefits that came with these changes. I learned at a very young age that, when you are willing to open your heart and accept others, anyone can become your family.

THE FAMILY OF GOD

We all desire to be a part of a family and to have a place where we feel we belong. God provides for that need and welcomes all to be a part of His family.

> *"Yet to all who received him,*
> *to those who believed in his name,*
> *He gave the right to become children of God."*
> JOHN 1:12

In Christ, we are a part of a very big and diverse family of brothers and sisters. Although I don't have any biological sisters, my life is filled with many sisters in Christ who are truly family to me. God's family of believers is intended to be a gift to us. This gift can be misunderstood, and the important role it plays in our lives is sometimes damaged. It is important to have an untainted understanding of the family of God and avoid placing unrealistic expectations on each other.

As the kids in God's family, we can all be defined as redeemed sinners, blessed by a Father who gives us gifts we don't deserve. We have all been adopted into the family of God and are learning to follow the "house rules." Although some of us have been in the family longer than others, we are all figuring out how things work in God's family. Even with the best of intentions, we all make mistakes and don't behave the way our Father would like us to.

It's safe to say that we aren't perfect, and it is very likely that we won't always do the right thing. For this reason, we can count on being disappointed by each other. When we look at each other in that light, it's easier to maintain more realistic expectations of one another and extend grace to each other.

Like the rest of us, maybe you have been hurt by one of your brothers or sisters in the family of God. At some point, someone has hurt all of us. Let's be honest, at times we have actually hurt someone else. Even though we sometimes hurt each other with our behavior, we all belong in the family of God, and we all share in the precious inheritance our Father has promised to us.

The best part of our family is our Father, God. Although, all the kids in the family occasionally mess up, we have a perfect Dad. Our Father is the King of kings, the Lord of lords, the great I AM, the creator of heaven and earth, and He chose us, all of us, to be His children through Christ.

> *"…the Spirit you received*
> *brought about your adoption to sonship.*
> *And by him we cry, 'Abba, Father.'"*
>
> ROMANS 8:15

This means we can call God our Daddy. It's a more intimate and personal title than Father. Although God is our Father and deserves our reverence and honor, he is also our Daddy. He is the one we can cry out to. He is intimately involved in our lives. He is the one who never leaves us or forsakes us. He never fails us, and when we fail, He still loves and accepts us. God's parental love towards us surpasses any human love we could ever experience. Even if you were fortunate enough to have the most wonderful earthly parents, nothing compares to the love our heavenly Father has for us.

I remember where I was the first time I really accepted the love God has for me as my Father. Up to that point in my life, I knew the Bible said that God is my Father, but it wasn't until one morning at a women's retreat that I believed and accepted that truth personally. I was sitting in the back of a large auditorium, and the speaker began to talk about her dad. She spoke of the wonderful man of God he was. She continued to explain that, during some of the most difficult times in life, her dad would always be there to share biblical words of encouragement and wisdom. Throughout her life, he always had words of hope to shower her with. She had countless memories of her earthly father washing her with the words of God.

I cried. They weren't tears of happiness and joy. I felt an overwhelming feeling of inadequacy. Thoughts of self-doubt filled my mind because I wasn't raised in a Christian home. Even in our broken home life, I always knew that my parents loved me. Although I appreciated and loved my earthly father, he never had words of biblical encouragement for me. I didn't have the kind of upbringing that this speaker had, and I began to wonder if God would ever be able to minister to others through me. I felt like a spiritual orphan. The words of the speaker began to completely fade to silence in my mind as I was consumed with discouragement. Then, God comforted me.

He whispered quietly to my heart, "You are not a spiritual orphan. I take you as my own. You are my daughter." God began to minister to me personally, just like the speaker described her earthly father did with her. God washed my insecure heart with his encouraging and comforting words. I was still crying, but my tears had turned from discouragement to hope. I found my identity in God through Christ Jesus. In that moment, I truly accepted the truth that I really am God's daughter.

I cried for three days following that retreat at the revelation of my newfound identity. I immediately went out and bought myself a new Bible and had it personalized with the words, "God's Daughter" on the cover. I searched through scriptures and memorized verses to help me hold on to this truth.

*"See what great love the Father has lavished on us,
that we should be called children of God!"*

1 JOHN 3:1

IDENTITY REMAINS
WHEN EVERYTHING ELSE CHANGES

God's definition of our identity is found in who He says we are, not merely in what we do. Often, we tend to determine our identity based on the things we do. On the surface, this seems right because the things we do should represent who we are. The problem with this perspective is that life is made up of many seasons. Seasons change—they come and go. With each new season of our lives, the things we do can change also. Sometimes, these changes can make us feel more valuable or less valuable as people based on what we are doing. Our value as people was never meant to be found in titles or positions or what we do but rather in who God says we are. God often uses change in our lives to remind us of the power of true identity.

"Yes, I am the vine, you are the branches."
JOHN 15:5

"Jesus Christ is the same yesterday, today and forever."
HEBREWS 13:8

Jesus reminds us that He is the secure, stable, never changing vine, and we are the branches. Branches change. They are exposed to the changing seasons. At times, the changes are uncomfortable and even scary, but as long as we remain in Him, our identity as God's children establishes us in the security of his unchanging and unconditional love.

For many years, a very large part of my identity was "Mom." It wasn't just what I did; that's who I was. Over the years and changing seasons of motherhood, I have learned that although I am a mom, my true identity is Child of God.

As moms, while we are raising our children, we love them, nurture them, pray for them, train them up, and watch over them so very sincerely. We pour our whole heart into our children, cherishing moments spent with them, rejoicing in every baby step they make and the milestones they accomplish. We bandage up the bumps and bruises, and we weep with tears only mommies can cry when it's a hurt we can't fix. Motherhood is an amazing journey. As our children grow, through the changing seasons of life, we will always be "Mom," but our roles need to change along the way. As our children mature into young adults, the time will eventually come to let our sweet ones test their wings and leave the security of the nest we have so diligently made for them. When this season of motherhood comes, it brings a change that most of us are not prepared for.

When the time came for our son to leave for college, I wasn't quite prepared for the mixed emotions I felt. Within a year, our daughter was ready to leave and start her life as well. I always said that if we did our parenting job right, we were raising them to be confident enough to leave us. It's a lot easier said than done. I was heartbroken. I knew it was a good change, a needed change, but I felt sad and insecure.

I remember, at the time, feeling a little lost. I was involved with lots of activities and ministry outside of the home, but it was still hard. I was used to my role as Nic and Katie's mom. I was a go-to person, a caregiver, and a guardian. It seemed like overnight the definition of "Mom" completely altered. When my role changed, it was a bit of an identity crisis for me. I was still "Mom," but my place in their lives was different. Kurt tried to be understanding with me, but it was definitely a more difficult transition for me than it was for him. Nic and Katie were patient with me during this time as I learned my new place in their adult world.

When we are raising our children and they are living at home, we have the privilege of being a part of their daily lives. We see them everyday. As they embrace the independence of adulthood, there is a transitional time when everyone is learning how to interact with each other. As parents, we need to learn new boundaries and respect for our children's adult lives. Actions that would once be considered responsible parenting could now be looked upon as an intrusion. Communication with my children during that time was crucial because my feelings could be hurt very easily.

I learned to embrace the temporary discomfort of that season, and it made way for the positive things God had planned for the future. I still get to be a go-to person for Nic and Katie, sometimes even a caregiver, and instead of guardian, I now enjoy the role of a confidant. Our son is getting ready to study for the LSAT test to enroll in law school, well on his way to accomplishing his dreams and calling in life. Our daughter is married—we have a wonderful son-in-law, a grandson, and a second grandbaby on the way. Grandchildren make that temporary empty nest season worth every single minute. People used to tell me, "Just wait until you have grandchildren; it's wonderful." They were right!

When everything around us changes and nothing feels familiar, we need to remember that God is our constant. He so faithfully holds us tight as the winds of change blow around us. We learn as we depend on Jesus, our secure and unchanging vine, that identity is found in who we are. Our value as people doesn't change just because our roles or responsibilities have changed. We are His. We are always God's children.

CHAPTER 7

Confidence

*"But blessed is the one who trusts in the Lord,
whose confidence is in Him."*

JEREMIAH 17:7

Confidence is a quality we all need in order to accomplish the extraordinary purpose that God has for each of us. The Lord's aspirations are always much bigger than we expect them to be. Usually, His plans are intimidating to us because it will take more than just self-confidence to achieve them. When certainty is dependent on our capability alone, we eventually reach a limitation. This is the point when we come to the end of our strength, courage, and abilities. Insecurity begins to set in because we feel incompetent to complete the task. Thoughts of insecurity can quickly lead to doubt and fear of failure. Eventually, we can find ourselves giving up on something we just barely started. When our courage is in God, there is never a point of limitation. Yes, there will always be obstacles, but never the absence of strength and ability to overcome those barriers. We can begin to reach our full, God-given potential in life when we look beyond our strength and tap into God's abilities through us.

BUILDING CONFIDENCE
BY FOLLOWING A SILLY DREAM

Have you ever had a dream that just seemed too silly to actually take seriously? Every week, I encourage people to pursue their dreams in life, especially the silly ones. My dream was to run a marathon, but every time I would think about it, I would quickly dismiss the thought with all the excuses I could think of: "That's ridiculous. I'm not a runner. I'm out of shape. I'm too overweight. I don't have time for that. I can't do that." Ten years ago, I finally decided to stop listening to all of the excuses. I had to ask myself the same question that I had asked so many others: "Do you believe that you can do everything through Christ who gives you strength?" I had believed that scripture many times before for spiritual and emotional strength. This time it was different. Was I willing to believe that Christ could help me with the *physical* strength to run a marathon?

CONFIDENCE TRAINS US
TO ACCOMPLISH OUR DREAMS

As I started the process, I quickly discovered that my confidence and faith in God wasn't going to be enough on its own. I was completely out of shape. When I told people about my dream and my decision to pursue it, the reactions were diverse. Most were very supportive, but some were very skeptical and doubtful. Many life lessons come with training to accomplish our dreams, even the silly ones. The first lesson I learned in training for my dream was to not listen to the skeptics. Having faith in God to accomplish anything through us means we have to believe God when He tell us we can, even when others doubt it.

Those who were supportive became a true inspiration to me. Although we have to tune out the doubters, we need other people to help us achieve a dream—and not only for the encouragement. Each person around us plays a unique role in the process. I was learning about running for the first time in my life. I continued to read and hear the same thing over and over, "Running is in the mind, and it is a mental challenge." I remember thinking, "If running is mental, and the Bible says that I have the mind of Christ, then *I'm set!*" The only problem with that concept was that I soon discovered that the *mind* of Christ is in *my* body, and my body was in no shape to run a marathon. I needed to get my body to a fitness level that could handle a marathon.

The next lesson learned was that pursuing my dream was not going to come easy. Perseverance was going to cost something, and the price was hard work. My confidence (faith) in God wasn't going to be enough on its own.

When I began training at thirty-seven years old, I had never run even one mile in my entire life, let alone 26.2 miles. Even in junior high, when it came to running the mile, I used to be the one in gym class who would run once, maybe twice, around the track and then walk the rest of the way. Now, it was literally decades later.

On my first official day of training, I could not run at all; I walked for twenty minutes. Slowly, day by day, I increased my walk time. Then, one day, I started to incorporate a *little* running, big emphasis on *little*. I would set markers for myself. At first, the markers were driveway to driveway or mail box to mail box. I would give myself incentives to keep running when I wanted to stop, "Just make it to that mailbox over there, then you can walk." The first day that I actually ran a mile without stopping, I plopped myself down on the curb and just soaked in the moment. I was so happy just to run a mile; you would have thought I had finished the actual marathon. Gradually, my goal markers went from being mailbox markers to mile markers. Don't be discouraged with small beginnings.

I had the best training partner anyone could ever have, God. His presence and strength always encouraged me and spurred me on. There were many days throughout my training when I thought of scriptures like 2 Chronicles 16:9: "For the eyes of the Lord range throughout the earth to strengthen those whose hearts are fully committed to Him." I would pray, "Oh, God, I hope your eyes on me because I could use some strength right about *now*!"

Confidence Is Bigger Than the Unexpected

Confidence that has been built with the wisdom of preparation can only truly succeed if its foundation is faith in God, who is always bigger than the unexpected. Even when we have diligently trained to reach our dreams, we will sometimes face situations that we aren't prepared for.

After fourteen months of physical and spiritual training, it was time to put all the hard work to the test. I lined up with thousands of other runners, ready to take on 26.2 miles; at my side was a friend, an experienced marathon runner who committed to run with me every step of the way. The announcer officially started the race, and I was on my way. I started off strong, filled with the joy of the moment, giving the crowd high-fives as I ran by. About mile five, I was doing great, still feeling really strong, but I noticed that it was already unusually hot outside. At mile eleven, I was all smiles as I saw my family and friends were there to cheer me on. At about mile thirteen, I realized the reason it felt so hot was because the temperature outside was in the high eighties and rapidly approaching the nineties. In spite of the exhausting heat, I found a tiny, little spurt of energy. With my friend helping me keep my pace, I began to speed it up just a little, not too much, just enough that I noticed myself passing groups of other runners.

By about mile sixteen, I was beginning to experience the first real signs of pain and fatigue. I had done lots of long distance training runs, but none of them had been in ninety-degree heat. I continued on. At mile nineteen, my family and friends were there once again to cheer me on. My kids jumped in to run next to me for a few yards. They encouraged me, "You can do it, Mom! You are doing great!" Then, my husband encouraged me and jumped in to run a few more yards with me. I found some encouragement to press on as other family members and friends clapped and cheered for me as I ran by. Mile twenty was a hard mile. They call it "the wall" because you feel like you just ran into one. That pretty much describes my experience with mile twenty.

Mile twenty-one was just ahead; I could see the banner. I noticed that I was out of Gatorade, so I decided to stop for a refill, and that's when the unexpected happened. As I stopped at the table, I completely blacked out. I could feel myself falling forward. I remember bracing my hands on my knees to keep myself from collapsing. I had all the signs of heat exhaustion. I was burning up, and I was shaking with the chills at the same time. I was nauseous and had the worst leg cramps I had ever experienced in my life. I felt delusional.

To help regain my mental focus, I remember saying to myself, "You're okay. You know your name and where you are…keep going." I couldn't bring myself to run anymore. It took everything I had just to walk. I felt defeated as I barely put one foot in front of the other. At this point, quitting had become a serious option. I thought, "It's not worth it. It's just a marathon." But, I knew that this experience was more than just a marathon for me. It was a dream that I trained and worked really hard for. I thought of the people who had pledged money to The Dream Center if I ran this marathon. I thought of the women at The Dream Center and all the obstacles in their lives that they fight to overcome to reach their dreams. I had to finish. At about mile twenty-five, the blood blister that had developed on my toe finally ruptured. Everything in my body was telling me to stop. I was so close to the finish line, and yet, the battle to quit raged inside of me.

The final life lesson that the marathon taught me was that all the hard work of training never really prepared me for the unexpected. Accomplishing my goal required that I dig deeper than I ever expected to do. God is always bigger than any unexpected challenge we face. Nothing is unexpected to God. I started saying out loud, "I'm *not* going to quit. I'm *not* going to quit. I'm *not* going to quit!" As I got closer to the finish, I forced myself to pick up the pace. Very slowly, I began to jog again, and my legs felt as though they were going to give out on me. Finally, the finish line was within reach. As they put the medal around my neck, I remember being filled with so much joy and thinking, "All things really are possible with God." Tens of thousands of people crossed the finish line that day. I'm sure that many of them did so without thinking of God.

To some, it was just another marathon; to me, it was an impossible dream that became a reality.

I always thought it was just a silly dream, but finishing the marathon allowed me to discover a brand new level of confidence in God. Not long after that race day, God began to speak to me about this book. Honestly, I know that I never would have had the confidence to begin seriously writing this book without the confidence training God gave me through the marathon.

Chapter 8

Perseverance

"...we count as blessed those who have persevered."

James 5:11

Our need to persevere is best exposed when we are up against opposition. Romans 5:3 tells us that suffering produces perseverance. This is only true of those who recognize their need to push through in the midst of their suffering. For some, suffering only produces a quitter's mentality. Second Peter 1:6 tells us to add perseverance to your self-control. Self-discipline goes hand in hand with perseverance. Self-indulgence satisfies only temporarily, but self-discipline yields true, lasting success. Self-indulgence is easier because it provides us with instant gratification. Self-discipline is harder and requires endurance and patience, but it yields long-term gratification. If we desire success in any area of our life, it takes perseverance.

When my husband and I started our own landscape business, we were also trying to dig our way out of massive debt. We had destroyed our credit due to poor money management, and we were attempting to build a new business. There weren't very many indulgences at that time in our lives. We had to continually say no to instant gratification and continue to be patient for the long-term goals we wanted to achieve. It took a lot of self-discipline and perseverance. Slowly, little by little, we paid off our debts and then began to build our credibility back up again. Week by week, month by month, and year by year, our business not only survived, it grew. True success can only come with self-discipline, working together with perseverance, and God's grace.

During the building years of our business, we lived in a small mobile home. This was a blessing at the time because it helped keep our financial overhead low, allowing us to continue to pay off our debt and build up the business. During our mobile home years, we made some of the sweetest memories and friendships anyone could ask for. It was our dream to buy a house of our own someday. I remember this felt more like a fantasy than a dream. Not only was our credit a complete mess, but we sold everything we could think of, including our family car, just to get the business started. I made regular visits to the pawn shop in those days to have money for groceries. Any profit that was made had to be put back into the business. There was equipment to purchase, insurances to secure, and employees to pay. Often, the needs of the business had to come before our own. There were times I wouldn't even let myself think about home ownership because it was so far out of reach—it was discouraging.

One day, we had a financial advisor come and speak with us. As we sat at a little kitchen table in our mobile home, she asked me, "If you could dream of living in any type of home, what would it be?" I sat there in my faded t-shirt and old shorts, looking at this very professionally dressed, polished woman, feeling a little intimidated; then, I said to her, "It's not just a dream. Someday, we will have a ranch with property." Have you ever said something and then immediately thought to yourself, "Did I say that out loud?" That's exactly how I felt the minute the words left my mouth. I believed that God could do it, but I also realized how ridiculous it sounded coming from someone in my situation, especially when you consider the fact that we live in southern California and ranch-style homes with property aren't easy to find or afford. It didn't help that she actually laughed at me.

Our desire for a home with property was a part of the plan we believed God had for our landscape business. Additionally, after living in a mobile home for so long, we really wanted a home that could be used to host events and be a blessing to others.

Staying on the course God set out for us took more perseverance and self-discipline than we ever could have expected. When the path seemed to get dark, God's promises were always there to shine encouraging light.

"And hope does not put us to shame, because God's love has been poured out into our hearts through the Holy Spirit, who has been given to us."
Romans 5:5

His hope never disappoints. The reason any of us persevere is to see our hope become a reality. God's promises keep hope alive while we persevere through challenges we are faced with.

We did our part, and God did His. Finally, seven years after starting the business, the day came—moving day! The day of our dreams had become a reality. We had the keys to our very own home. No, it wasn't a ranch house; it was actually an average size house, but it didn't matter to us. We were home owners! That night we slept soundly, enjoying the fruit of our long labor. Life seemed bright and joyful.

The next morning, our bright skies turned dark when my husband went to our business office only to find that we had been robbed. Almost all of our equipment was stolen. While we slept in our new home for the first time, our business was being robbed of everything we had worked seven years to build. We had an insurance policy, but we didn't have the extra package on the policy to cover the stolen equipment. We had to replace everything that was stolen ourselves.

We had already persevered for seven years to build our business the first time. This time we needed the perseverance to *rebuild* our business. It felt a lot like we would have to start all over. There were moments I feared all of our perseverance was in vain. I feared we would lose our house and the business and be left with nothing. The only true place of comfort and hope was God's promises. These promises helped me overcome my fears. Later that night, my husband rallied the troops together. He sat our family down at the dinner table and said, "Well, we've been hit, that's for sure! It was a direct hit, and it's going to hurt, but we're not sunk! We'll be fine." I knew when he said that he had no idea how we would make it, but his positive words of faith gave us hope to press on. With the strength we found in God's promises, we started the rebuilding process. Within six months, we had replaced almost all of the equipment that previously took seven years to accumulate.

We had just barely replaced all the stolen equipment, and we were robbed again. This time, they took even more than they did the first time. The second robbery felt like a death blow. I cried for a whole day. Could this be happening again? It felt unreal. Usually, in our marriage, if one of us is down, the other is up. Not this time. That day, both of us seriously contemplated quitting and closing the business doors. One by one, friends, family, and even our employees surrounded us with encouragement to press on.

Later that evening, we decided to rebuild yet again. As we stood in the empty garage, we didn't know how we would be able to replace the equipment again. We lifted our prayers to God. Although there was no real evidence of hope yet, we thanked God in advance for His help to fill the empty garage with equipment once again. Over time, we were able to replace what was stolen and increase our inventory larger than it ever was before we were robbed.

Since the second robbery, we have moved again, and yes, this time into a ranch-style home with two and one-half acres of property. It perfectly meets all the needs of our business with plenty of room to be a blessing to others. We've hosted youth camp outs, carnivals, ministry outreaches, engagement parties, numerous weddings (one of them was our daughter's), birthday parties, holiday parties, baby showers, prayer meetings, and baptisms in our pool. The property has even been used to film a couple of music videos. Lots of fun memories of laughter and even a few tears from very special moments have filled our home. We've been in our ranch property for over ten years now.

Doesn't that sound like a happy ending to my story of perseverance? It was a happy ending to that season, but it was also the beginning of another perseverance story. Not long after we moved in to our ranch property, the economy started to slow down, affecting the income for our landscape business. Within the first two years after the move, our business sales dropped by half, and we lost half the equity in our property. Once again, we were faced with obstacles to overcome with faith and endurance. I've learned that when you are persevering toward a goal, once that goal is achieved, the perseverance continues with something else. This gives us the opportunity to live our lives continually trusting God. The gift of perseverance is not found in the temporary happiness of reaching a goal but rather in the character and hope it produces in us to keep moving forward to the next goal and the next after that.

> *"You need to persevere so that when you have done the will of God, you will receive what he has promised."*
> HEBREWS 10:36

Perseverance is a huge part of every success story. If we desire success in any area of our lives, it takes perseverance. Dreams in our heart cannot become a reality without perseverance. Ultimately, when we have the hope of heaven in our hearts, we know that all our endurance in this life will conclude with the bliss of eternal, heavenly paradise.

CHAPTER 9

Joy

*"I have told you this so that my joy may be in you
and that your joy may be complete."*

JOHN 15:11

Happiness is often based on our circumstances; joy is a steady, inner strength that has the ability to surpass and override our most discouraging situations. Joy is actually the tool God has provided to help us through the hardships of life, and yet, oddly, it is usually the first thing we let go of when life gets hard.

CHOOSING JOY THAT IS BASED ON GOD'S PROMISES

"The Joy of the Lord is your strength."

NEHEMIAH 8:10

As a young Christian woman, I remember observing God's joy in a very dear woman in our church. She always wore a smile. When I'd greet her and ask the typical question, "How are you?" *every time* she would respond the same way and say, "Wonderfully blessed, praise God!" I remember thinking to myself, "Wow, she is always happy! Life must be pretty good for her." As I matured and got to know her, I realized that it wasn't happiness that kept that beautiful smile on her face, and it wasn't because she never had trials. The reason she could respond with the same completely genuine heart was because the joy of the Lord had truly become her strength. The more I thought about this, I realized that she was intentionally choosing to speak truth in spite of her current feelings. The truth of God's promise is that no matter what we have currently going on, *we are blessed.*

> *"Blessed are those whose strength is in you [God]…"*
> PSALM 84:5

> *"Blessed are all who take refuge in Him."*
> PSALM 2:12

> *"Blessed is he whose transgressions are forgiven,*
> *whose sins are covered."*
> PSALM 32:1

I gave myself a challenge many years ago to deliberately respond with, "I'm blessed," when people ask how I am doing. I have not mastered that response as beautifully as the dear woman who taught me that lesson in life, but I continue to make the effort to implement this little reminder into my day.

WE CAN'T BLAME OTHERS FOR OUR LACK OF JOY

> *"So then, each of us will give*
> *an account of ourselves to God."*
> ROMANS 14:12

We are responsible for our own lives, attitudes, and behaviors. No one can take our joy away from us; however, we have the ability to forfeit it. It's important to remember that we can't control the lives of others; they stand before God himself to give a personal account for their actions. Likewise, we will stand before God and give a personal account of our own. Therefore, we shouldn't let the actions, words, or attitudes of others have power to control us.

This is a little exercise I like to do to help me remember that I am personally responsible for myself and have no control over the actions of others. First, I hold my hand in front of my face. Next, with the other hand, I point my finger in the space between my face and my hand then say, "Everyone on this side of the hand, I can control." Let that sink in for a minute. I am the only one on that side of my hand. One of the fruits of the Spirit of God is self-control. God has given us the power of control, but only insofar as it is concerning ourselves.

Lastly, while my one hand is still held up in front of my face, I move my finger from the space between my hand and my face to the other side of the hand and say, "Everyone on this side of the hand, I can't control."

There are a lot of people on the other side of our hand who we love very much. There are many others who are important to us. Their actions, words, and attitudes impact our lives. We can't control their choices, and it's not our job to try convicting them or judging them either. They are as responsible to God for themselves as we are personally responsible for how we respond to them. Our response is to love people and trust God. We will hold onto our joy and not relinquish it when we learn to take responsibility for our part and let go of the things that are out of our control.

CHAPTER 10

Hope

*"Be strong and take heart,
all you who hope in the Lord."*

PSALM 31:24

Hope is more than a human need. I believe it is truly essential to an effective existence. Nothing is quite as bleak as hopelessness. My all-time favorite movie is *It's a Wonderful Life*. The movie begins with the sounds of prayers reaching the heavens for George Bailey. After hearing the prayers, God calls for Clarence, the angel, to help George Bailey in his time of need. Clarence asks God, "Is he sick?" God answers, "Worse, he's discouraged." Although George Bailey was faced with a financial problem in the movie, the true crisis was his perspective. The entire second half of the movie is all about God giving George Bailey a new perspective—one that leads to hope instead of discouragement.

When our hope dies, it's as though a light goes out in our soul, and everything in our lives becomes tainted with an outlook of despair. It is at these desolate moments in our life that one might ask the question, "Where are you, God? Are you even real?" I have been guilty of asking such questions. I have felt that struggle within my heart.

"Before they call I will answer,
while they are still speaking I will hear."
ISAIAH 65:24

In times of hopelessness, it is the most difficult to be comforted by the words of God because our lack of hope makes it so hard to believe that God's beautiful promises are true. I know it's hard, but cry out to God anyway! In my darkest hours, God has always revealed Himself to me, in spite of my faithless and shameful attitudes. Be assured. God *is* real, and He is always only a heart's cry away. He hears you. He sees you. He knows you.

UNDERWATER

Life's trials don't seem to come just one at a time. If they hit your life the same way they do mine, they come relentlessly one right after the other. It can feel like you're underwater, swimming as hard as you can to break through the surface, and just as you gasp a deep breath of air, you are pulled under again. It happens over and over again; with each plunge downward, exhaustion and despair begin to take your hope. It doesn't matter who you are or the positions and titles you hold; it doesn't matter how long you have walked with God or how much faith you have—if life's trials rock your world hard enough and long enough, anyone can lose sight of hope and find themselves underwater in discouragement.

There was a time a while back that felt like I was underwater more than I was surfacing for air. My brother was going through a personal crisis that required a lot of help, my son was dealing with a very serious medical condition, and our business was experiencing huge financial trouble. I would wake up every day trying to convince myself it was going to be okay, but the emptiness inside made me painfully aware of how overwhelmed and lost I felt.

Time has passed since then. All of the trials that seemed so devastating in the moment have been resolved. My brother overcame that very difficult time in his life. My son recovered from the medical challenge he faced, and our financial situation didn't turn out to be as devastating as it initially seemed. I wonder sometimes what would it be like if I could go back in time and talk myself through that rough patch? I would be able to tell myself all about how God never left me and how He provided for every single need. However, since then, other trials have come, so I would have to tell myself about all of those too. Hope cannot be based upon our circumstances because situations change, sometimes daily. When we are overwhelmed and discouraged, we need hope that is stronger than the current problem in front of us and unshakable in the midst of adversity.

"Be assured. God is real, and He is always only a heart's cry away. He hears you. He sees you. He knows you."

FIVE WAYS TO HELP OVERCOME DISCOURAGEMENT AND FIND HOPE AGAIN

1. **Believe that God is always there for you**

2. **Don't follow negativity or bad advice—trust God**

3. **Choose to live in an atmosphere that encourages your faith**

4. **Let God heal the broken areas of your life**

5. **Let hope restore your dreams and your vision**

Believe that God is always there for you

*"May the God of hope fill you with all joy and peace
as you trust Him so that you may overflow
with hope by the power of the Holy Spirit."*

ROMANS 15:13

Even though we don't always see it, God Himself has made a way for us to find hope again. He promises to always be right there with us, and He never leaves our side through the process. The Holy Spirit of God is not only with us but also with*in* us. The Holy Spirit is a true companion. He walks with us and talks with us. As I was pondering this, the thought came to me, "Right now, while the Holy Spirit is with me, leading me, comforting me through whatever I am facing in life, He is also, at the very same moment, holding someone else who may be challenged with something far more devastating than my current circumstances." I was so humbled by God's unconditional love for each of us personally. He never compares our lives' situations to others'. He doesn't prioritize and decide who needs Him more. He is faithful with *all* who call on Him because He loves us all, and He keeps his promises. This awesome reality of God's nature is a true encouragement to our soul.

"The LORD himself goes before you
and will be with you; he will never leave you nor
forsake you. Do not be afraid; do not be discouraged."
DEUTERONOMY 31:8

The word "discouraged" means to weaken stamina and zeal, to prevent, restrain, depress. In this scripture, God is telling us, "Because I go before you, because I am always with you, do not let anything steal away your zeal and stamina for life and your life's purpose. Do not let anything restrain or depress you. I am with you, and I will never leave you."

Depression is a growing problem worldwide. We all have temporary feelings of discouragement. If we try to simply ignore the feelings, discouraging thoughts have the tendency to build up over time. God is there to help us battle the discouraging thoughts before they reach the depths of depression.

God has lavished His love upon us. It's in our times of discouragement that we need to remind ourselves of His love more than ever. Jeremiah 31:3 says, "…I have loved you with an everlasting love…" Gently, I close my eyelids and place my hands over my heart as if to say, "Listen, hold tightly to the words you are about to hear. Hold them close to you." My mouth forms the words I have spoken over myself countless times before, "My God loves me." I remind myself of His everlasting love and encourage myself to believe in the power of these words, "My God loves me."

The Holy Spirit wants to walk with us through the joys of life and be a very present help in our times of discouragement. As we trust Him, God has made overflowing hope available to us by the power of the Holy Spirit. As we lift our hands, giving all our concerns to God and believing that He truly is always with us, our hope is renewed.

Don't follow negativity or bad advice—trust God

"Do not be misled:
'Bad company corrupts good character.'"

1 CORINTHIANS 15:33

The Bible tells us not to be misled. Our diligent efforts to hold onto hope can be led astray with constant negativity or bad advice from others. During times of despair, we need to carefully choose the people we are listening to. The people we are surrounding ourselves with can have an effect on our attitude. We don't always have control over the negative opinions of others; however, we always have the power to choose whether or not we will listen to them.

I spoke earlier about a time in my life when I felt "underwater." My perspective became more and more jaded during that time. Negativity and hopelessness slowly began to creep into my life. My thoughts, words, and actions didn't align with my faith in God. At that point in my life, it would have been easy to gravitate toward others who were also discouraged and struggling with negativity. It was much harder to vulnerably expose my hopeless outlook on life to those who I knew would challenge my bleak perspective. However, that was exactly what I needed. No one needs to stay in his despair too long.

If discouragement seems to be hanging on a while, we should definitely ask ourselves, "Who am I spending time with? Are these people encouraging me to hold onto hope or not?" As we honestly assess our surroundings, we need to ask God for help in making any changes that may need to be made. Sometimes, we need to change our environment, including the places we go and the groups we are involved in. If the negativity is coming from someone we live with, this can make it more difficult; however, ultimately, we have the final decision regarding how we will respond to those around us. We have a choice to make. Who will we listen to? Will we listen to the discouraging negativity of others, or will we choose to believe in the promises of God?

Choose to live in an atmosphere that encourages your faith

"Therefore, brothers, in all our distress and persecution we were encouraged about you because of your faith."

1 Thessalonians 3:7

When we're discouraged or deeply disappointed, we have to resist the urge to isolate ourselves. Solitude seems like a good idea because we might not feel like interacting with anyone, but truthfully, withdrawing is a trap that is more likely to keep us in despair even longer.

Also, during that "underwater" time, hopelessness flooded my mind with a tainted point of view. I was grouchy and short tempered. Often, I found myself responding to others with shameful outbursts. It left a trail of embarrassing behavior and countless apologizes. It got to the point that I found myself purposefully avoiding close interaction with others. I genuinely felt like I didn't have anything good to offer. As I felt myself gradually spiraling downward, I heard the gentle voice of God in my heart telling me to stay connected. Everything in me wanted to stop serving in the church, curl up, and go away, but I didn't. I continued to teach Bible studies, although I cried through every single one. I vulnerably talked about my process of reconciling God's promises with the discouragement I felt. Resisting the temptation to disappear played an intricate role in overcoming discouragement in my life.

Intentional socialization in an uplifting environment is good for a broken heart. It's the exact opposite of the way we feel, but when we push through and purposefully get involved with other faith-filled people, we will discover that encouragement slowly finds its way to our heart. It's important to enforce a positive and hopeful atmosphere. Positive influences are invaluable when we are attempting to discover hope again. Choosing to read encouraging books and listening to inspiring, faith-filled messages can also help us develop an uplifting atmosphere that will inspire our faith. Often, God uses others to help us find our way to hope again.

Let God heal the broken areas of your life

"Nevertheless, I will bring health and healing to it;
I will heal my people and will let them enjoy
abundant peace and security."

JEREMIAH 33:6

No matter how long we may have lived with pain or hurt, God desires to "bring health and healing to it" and restore us to a place of "abundant peace and security." God is ready; we just have to be willing to let Him into those painful places deep inside. It's hard to be vulnerable, mostly because we don't want to think about the pain. Finding hope is worth it. God heals every broken place that He touches.

I have found that anger and hope don't coexist well together. Part of the healing process is to lay down our anger. Maybe we need to work through some forgiveness as we discussed in chapter 1. It can also just simply be a conscious decision to let go of an angry disposition. Anger and aggression can be used as a false sense of security—as if they will protect our heart from being broken again.

One of the main reasons for my emotional outbursts during that time of discouragement was anger. I was hurting and so overwhelmed from the circumstances in my life that I literally took an entire day off so that I could lay everything out before God. Tired of the way I felt, I knew that I needed God to intervene and heal my heart. As I poured out every disappointment and question I had to God, He patiently listened and mended my brokenness with His powerful compassion. His love began to soften the rough edges that the anger had formed around my heart. I found strength as His love taught me to trust Him with all the uncertainties before me. Although none of my circumstances instantly changed, my perspective did.

Anger is unsettling and provoking. God offers genuine peace that permeates from the depths of our soul outward. Making a choice to voluntarily lay down our shield of anger and exchange it for true security found in trusting God can often be the beginning of hope once again.

Let hope restore your dreams and your vision

*"For I know the plans I have for you,' declares the
Lord, 'plans to prosper you and not to harm you,
plans to give you hope and a future.'"*

JEREMIAH 29:11

Has discouragement robbed your dreams? Hope is fuel for pursuing our dreams. Hopelessness tends to be a dream killer. When we feel hopeless, it's as if we are just going through the motions of life. Here's the good news: even when discouragement has caused us to lose sight of our future hope, God still clearly sees the plans He has for us. It may temporally feel like your dreams are gone, but they aren't—God's got them, and He is ready to share them with you. Your God loves you, and He loves the dreams in your heart.

God led me from survival mode to a place of boundless inspiration. Discouragement produced a nearsighted outlook filled with temporal fear. Although hopelessness tried to take away my God-given ambition in life, hope breathed creativity and purpose back into my life.

The Bible tells us that God is love (1 John 4:16), and it also tells us that love always hopes (2 Corinthians 13:7)—God *is* love and love *always* hopes. He has an endless supply of hope for us when we need it. When God breathes hope into our lives, He replaces the sluggish perspective of discouragement with a zeal and excitement for life. No matter how dim the light of hope gets, He can revive our hope and vision. The hope that God has for us is not limited by our ability to have hope for ourselves. He is the very source of hope.

CHAPTER 11

Courage

*"Be on your guard; stand firm in the faith;
be courageous; be strong."*

1 CORINTHIANS 16:13

Fear is a real challenge we all face, everything from paralyzing panic to daily worry and stress. Although the range of experience may differ, we are all confronted with anxiety. Many sleepless nights have been spent, many dreams unfulfilled, and many opportunities missed all because of fear. To have courage doesn't mean fear doesn't exist—courage is the strength and conviction that something else is more important than the fear we have. So, when God tells us to be on guard, stand firm, be courageous, and be strong, He knows that, along the way, we will eventually be antagonized with fear. His courage calls to us to dig deep, with faith beyond the angst we feel, to a place where we can dare to believe in victory over it. What lies ahead of us on the other side of the fears that hold us captive? Life. Not only the experience of living but living in such a bold way that fulfills our God-given purpose.

SPIRITUAL PROTECTION

*"My prayer is not that you take them out of the world,
but that you protect them from the evil one."*

JOHN 17:15

God knows that we need His protection to help us stand with courage in this life. Jesus prayed for us, "...not that You would take them out of the world, but that You protect them from the evil one." The evil one that Jesus spoke of is still very actively filling our world with as much wicked behavior as he possibly can. Although God has already defeated our enemy (Revelation 12:12), Satan is filled with fury because he knows that his time here is limited.

Just watching the evening news and witnessing the devastating stories, we realize that Satan is very busy in this world we live in. As believers, we are here to be the light of God in a world filled with darkness. Fear will dim the lamp of God's influence through us. Trusting in God's love replaces the anxiety with a bright light of confident faith. Imagine, just for a moment, how dark it would be here if all the lights of God were gone. Jesus prayed that God would not take us out of this world but rather keep us a part of it and protect us, knowing that we are designed and destined to be light in the midst of darkness.

*"For he will command his angels concerning you to
guard you in all your ways."*

PSALM 91:11

It is likely that we will never know, on this side of eternity, how often God's angels intervene on our behalf. Occasionally, we will find ourselves in a dangerous situation and know that, somehow, God's angels were there to help us through. Most of the time, angels are guarding us in ways we don't see.

As a pastoral counselor, I often hear people genuinely question, "Why didn't God and His angels protect me from that bad thing that happened to me?" God is good. His plans for all of us are for good and not for harm. Victimizing people with cruelty is *never* a part of God's plan for anyone. Sin entered this world through the will of man and deception of the enemy. God has given to us free will; we are not puppets on His string. He lovingly gives us His truth to guide our way, but we all have the power to choose. Unfortunately, sin still enters our world through the will of man and the deception of the enemy. Sinful behavior that has been encouraged by the darkness of Satan will always leave a trail of trauma and deep pain. God already has a plan in place to heal the pain and restore all traumatic situations we have lived through. For everything that the enemy has planned to harm us, God is prepared to heal and redeem it for our good.

With the prayers of Jesus covering us and the angels of heaven protecting us, we can find the courage to illuminate this world with the love of Christ. God always has a rescue plan in place for us, and He will be our hiding place when we need one. Encouraged by all the promises of God, we can confidently face all unknowns and storms of life and rest in the arms of His protection.

UNDERSTANDING AND USING THE ARMOR OF GOD

God has equipped us with everything we need to stand firm as His light against the darkness of Satan. The Bible describes this equipment as pieces of armor.

*"Stand firm then, with the belt of **truth** buckled around your waist, with the breastplate of **righteousness** in place, and with your feet fitted with the readiness that comes from the gospel of **peace**. In addition to all this, take up the shield of **faith**, with which you can extinguish all the flaming arrows of the evil one. Take the helmet of **salvation** and the sword of the Spirit, which is the **word of God**. And pray in the Spirit on all occasions with all kinds of **prayers** and requests. With this in mind, be alert and always keep on praying for all the Lord's people."*

EPHESIANS 6:14–18

Although the pieces of armor can serve as a helpful reminder of God's spiritual protection, it is most important to remember the actual gifts of God that the pieces of armor represent.

Let's look at them again, this time in different order:

- We hear the *truth*.
- We believe and know the *truth* by *faith*.
- Through *faith* we receive *salvation*.
- God's *salvation* through Christ Jesus gives us *righteousness*.
- Christ's *righteousness* gives us *peace* with God.
- Because God has given us *truth, faith, salvation, righteousness,* and *peace*, we are prepared to use our weapon against the evil one. That weapon is the *Word of God*. We speak God's Word and have victory over the lies of the enemy.
- We are committed to *prayer*! We pray on all occasions, according to the *Word of God*.

Do you see the gospel at work in this sequence? Through the gospel of Jesus Christ, God has provided us all we need to stand firm and protected against the darkness and wickedness of our enemy, Satan.

AM I USING GOD'S SPIRITUAL PROTECTION?

Each piece of God's armor provides a spiritual reminder of the personal ways God has provided so perfectly for each of us to recognize and overcome the tactics of the enemy. God provides light for our path, helping us to focus on His direction in spite of the constant distractions we encounter as we walk through life. The darkness holds no power in the presence of God's holy and perfect light. As we travel through this life, we all get weary and feel as though we are not able to stand firm. The questions on the following page provide a quick heart check and will help us to take up our spiritual protection again.

*"God has provided
all we need to stand firm."*

AM I USING GOD'S SPIRITUAL PROTECTION?

- **Truth:** Am I listening to God's truth in my life, or am I listening to lies?

- **Faith:** When I hear the truth of God, do I really believe His truth? Am I partnering with God to daily strengthen my faith?

- **Salvation:** Do I have the joy of God's salvation? Is the passion of my first love for Christ alive in my life? Am I believing in the freedom Christ died and rose for me to have?

- **Righteousness:** Am I seeing myself the way God sees me? Have I accepted the righteousness of Christ to cover me? Do I believe that I have right standing with God? Am I embracing my new identity in Christ?

- **Peace:** Do I have God's peace in my life? Does His peace give me readiness and confidence in the midst of the battles in life, or am I stressed out and afraid?

- **Word of God:** Do I read the Bible? Do I believe it is the Word of God? Am I applying and sharing God's Word in my life? Am I speaking out loud the truth of God's Word as my weapon against the enemy when he comes against me?

- **Prayer:** Am I spending time communicating with God? Am I praying for God's insight and direction for my personal life? Am I praying for others?

Light Stands

*"Neither do people light a lamp and put it under a
bowl. Instead they put it on its stand, and it gives
light to everyone in the house."*

MATTHEW 5:15

God's amazing light continually dispels the darkness, not
only for our own personal benefit but also to share with those
around us. We are designed to be beacons, helping others discover God's love, which leads all to a fulfilled life.

God has uniquely placed opportunities of influence in each
of our lives to become light stands to shine for Him. These can
be public stands, and they are also in our personal lives. We
have many of them. I may have the public light stands as an
author, pastor, mentor, and Bible study teacher, but equally, I
have been given the personal light stands of wife, mom, nana,
friend, daughter, and sister. Each stand has been entrusted to
us to serve with the love and light of God. Fanning the flames
of our faith and keeping God's light burning strong within us
is destined for so much more than merely ourselves.

Turn on the Light

*"I have come into the world as a light, so that no one
who believes in me should stay in darkness."*

JOHN 12:46

Have you ever noticed that we have lights everywhere? We
have streetlights, indoor and outdoor house lights, and interior
and exterior automobile lights. We even have lights on our
phones, just in case we happen to be somewhere that doesn't
have light. As soon as it gets dark, we start turning on the

lights because we don't like the dark. Here's an interesting thought: as much as we clearly don't like the dark, we don't try to fight the dark to conquer it. We don't worry about the dark; we just turn on the light. We have learned to trust a little electrical light switch to be powerful enough to overcome the dark for us. Spiritual darkness can be defeated just as easily. We don't have to worry about it or fight with it—we just need to learn to trust Jesus. The same way we trust a light switch to dispel physical darkness, we need to depend on Jesus to be our spiritual light and overcome any spiritual darkness in our life. The next time you find yourself in a dark place, just turn on the light.

CHAPTER 12

Comfort

"My comfort in my suffering is this:
Your promise preserves my life."

PSALM 119:50

Sometimes life hurts; emotional pain is often worse than physical. When the heart aches with grief, God is there to comfort. We do not always have the answers to all of our questions, but we do have hope that our heart can heal with the anointing of Jesus Christ.

"The Spirit of the Sovereign Lord is on me,
because the Lord has anointed me…
He has sent me to bind up the brokenhearted."

ISAIAH 61:1

God ministers to us through Christ Jesus in a very precious way, with deep healing of every broken place. The Bible says that God sent Jesus to "bind" up the broken hearted. To "bind" is to bandage up a wound. Have you ever had to bandage a cut for a little child? It usually requires some time to convince the child to let you do it first. He or she squirms and tries to keep the wounded area away from you. Why? Because it hurts, and the child knows to bandage it means you have to touch it and clean it first. No one ever really wants to expose a painful area to touch, but that is exactly what is needed. Binding up a wound is a hands-on experience. Jesus has healing in His hands, ready to bring wholeness and restoration. We have to be willing to let Him in, exposing the painful places to Him, and then, we have to be willing to receive His comfort.

One of the greatest privileges I have is providing pastoral care and counseling at The Dream Center. I use the word "privilege" because I consider the heart of a person to be Holy Spirit territory. It is within the heart that the Spirit of God heals with deep compassion. To be a trusted partner with the Holy Spirit and lead someone in emotional and spiritual healing is a priceless experience. There is a beauty that is hard to describe, that is discovered in the eyes of someone when the layers of sorrow and despair give way to powerful healing under God's gentle touch. I have seen the beauty that God can bring when we let Him comfort us.

There are many reasons we may experience grief. When hardship visits us, it's not productive to compare our pain with someone else's. God doesn't do that; He understands us completely and brings personalized healing uniquely designed for each person.

COMFORT WHEN WE MOURN

*"God blesses those who mourn,
for they will be comforted."*

MATTHEW 5:4

Death of a loved one is heartbreaking. Aching throbs from inside of you that begs to be comforted. There are moments in the grieving process when words and hugs from those around us can temporarily help to relieve the pain. And other times there are no words or comfort from any human effort that can help. Only the blessing of God's comfort is able to reach far enough into the depth of places no one else can see to restore. God never promised that we wouldn't mourn, but He did say that when we do, He would be there to comfort us.

It was a Tuesday morning, much like many others before. Every detail of it is engraved in my mind. I looked down at my phone and read a text message that would not only change the course of the day, but my life forever. My mom was in the ER and was going into emergency heart surgery. I called her immediately. I was happy to hear her voice, yet saddened by the pain I heard behind her words. My voice was shaking as I tried to encourage her.

After her surgery, I held my mom's hand, and she held mine with a faint squeeze. Too weak to speak, but with her love, she acknowledged me. The doctor and nurses tried to help me understand. My head spun, trying to take it in. Words like heart, ruptured, bleeding—it was too much for my mind to handle. Just after my brother arrived at the hospital, mom held our hands, and with her very last bit of strength, she intentionally mouthed the words, "I love you." Then, she directed her eyes toward heaven, prayed softly, and left us. They quickly moved us out of the room. The medical crash carts were brought in; dozens of doctors and nurses tried to bring her back. But I knew, as I stood out in the hallway, my mom was no longer on this side of eternity. She had crossed over into paradise with Jesus. It was one of the most painful things, yet one of the most beautiful things, I have ever experienced in my life.

Only hours after receiving that unexpected text message, my mom was gone. I felt numbness from the shock. Yet, far beneath the numbness was peace. I know that, without that deep-down peace from God, I would have teetered on the edge. The best way to describe it is a gentle strength that held me and steadied my way. Peace is the first gift that God's comfort brought me in the initial moments of my grief, and His peace continued to carry me through the mourning process.

Early the next morning, I felt the void of loss and, at the same time, the pressure of all the details and arrangements that needed to be made. When someone very close to you passes, there are a lot of things that require your attention. I sat at my computer, attempting to complete one of the tasks on my long list of things that had to be addressed that day. I could feel it coming like a roaring avalanche getting ready to give way. It started in my heart and then gushed out of me in sobs of deep pain. My mind, body, and soul were consumed in uncontrollable crying. I wasn't sure how those painful tears would stop or how I was going to pull it together long enough to accomplish anything at all. God's comfort slowly and so gently began to settle me. Although His comfort is soft, it isn't weak. His comfort brings amazing strength. God's comfort makes us strong in the midst of our weakness. He gives us strength to make it through situations that we never thought we could. This strength that He gives builds inside of us, helping us continue on with life after deep and painful loss. He helps us to move forward when we don't understand and when we don't want to.

In the months that followed, I continued to be pulled to and fro with the demands and obligations of my own life and wrapping up my mom's affairs. In the midst of it all, sometimes I just didn't want to do it. I missed her. Only a month after her death, I had to make sure her apartment was completely cleaned out and give the keys to the manager.

I stood in her apartment. Her loved ones had gone through her things and selected keepsakes to remember her by. All that remained were piles of mess scattered over her apartment. I quickly got busy to get the job done, but I began to feel an attitude rise up within me. This mess was once my mom's home. It was the place where she lived and laughed and loved. Now, it was just heaps of things and my task at hand. Her death was so sudden; she was so young. Oh, how I wanted her there instead of this awful job. Sometimes, the things that life requires of us are not at all fun or easy. My attitude got worse by the minute.

As I scurried around, I heard the still, soft voice of God speak to my heart, "Come, sit with me a while." The pressure of the deadline before me tempted me to ignore His voice. But, I know His voice. I have heard Him call me many times, so I accepted His invitation. I sat on mom's stairs and gazed through the open front door at the beautiful day God had made. I heard the sounds of life around me: birds singing, breeze in the trees. My heart found peace once again in the arms of God. I am so thankful that God loved me enough to give me a much-needed time out that day.

I exchanged my frustration and bad attitude for the comfort of God and found strength to continue on. Cleaning mom's house and giving her keys back to the manager provided more closure as I said goodbye to my mom here on this earth until we see each other again in heaven. There have been many life moments since then, and I would have loved to share them all with her. I miss her. Yet, her passing has placed an even stronger hope of heaven in my heart. The pain of my loss is always met with the overwhelming peace found in God's promise of eternal life. I know that I will see her again.

Somehow, knowing that helps me to release her to God and embrace the beauty of my life that is daily unfolding before me—without her.

It was God's comfort that made it possible for me to walk through the pain of losing my mom. God is full of compassion, and He is always reaching out to us to heal and comfort our wounds. We must be willing to respond to his efforts. When our heart hurts, we have a choice to make. We can either hold so tightly to the pain that our heart will grow hard, or we can respond to God's love and let Him carry us through comfort to healing.

CHAPTER 13

Living Fulfilled

*"...I have come that they may have life
and have it to the full."*

JOHN 10:10

Living a full life usually has a small beginning. A big, beautiful tree was once a tiny seed. It can only reach its full potential with the nourishment of soil, refreshing water, and the warmth of sunshine. Just like the tree that started as a seed, inside of everyone's heart is an undeveloped seed filled with potential. Sometimes, it is hidden deep within so that human eyes cannot see. God sees the seed of promise He has placed within us. It has been designed perfectly by Him to come to full fruition. We believe that we have a purpose, but we need encouragement to grow. Feeling comfortable beneath the surface, we are tempted to remain safely hidden under the soil until God showers our heart with His nourishing Word. The light of His Son brings warmth and comforts us. Life begins to spring up. Filled with a dream, we begin to grow, slowly at first, until just the right time; then, we emerge, no longer hidden. The time has come to break forth and arise. Undiscovered potential becomes reality. It feels like a vulnerable and fragile time, and yet, there is boldness and confidence found in the unfailing love of God. Every day, there are seeds of potential within us and others around us trying to burst forth into life.

So Much More Than We Can Imagine

How should we determine our potential in life? Some would say our potential is based on the education we have. Others say it is whom we know or the environment that we were raised in. Still, others think demographics like gender, age, and economic status are substantial determining factors to one's potential. Although each of these can play a role in forming human guidelines, God's Word tells us that He is able to do so much more than we can imagine.

"Now to him who is able to do immeasurably more than all we ask or imagine, according to his power that is at work within us, to him be glory in the church and in Christ Jesus throughout all generations, forever and ever! Amen."

Ephesians 3:20–21

We find a new level of fullness in life when we see God's potential rather than focusing on the limiting factors in our own lives or the lives of others around us. I have come to realize and truly believe that the only way we can live completely fulfilled lives is to allow God to define and outline our lives and then lead us in them. God is limitless. Our potential is whatever God says our potential is. His definitions of who we are and what He has called us to do will always seem much fuller than we could have imagined. Believing that we really are God's children and that He genuinely desires to fill our lives to overflowing completeness is only the beginning. We must be willing to face the limits we have placed on ourselves, and then, with God's strength, run straight through them.

The status quo is defined as the existing state or condition. Each one of us has our own current status quo. Every day, you and I will be faced with lethargic mindsets trying to tell us that it is okay to settle. The Holy Spirit reminds us that we can live beyond that mentality because God is so much bigger than the status quo. On our journey to discover our fulfilled life in Christ, we will all be tempted with the tendency to embrace the status quo around us. If we really want to live the God-defined life we are hoping for, we have to push through our current condition and reach out further than we ever thought we could.

Have you been hearing that soft, yet challenging voice of God calling you to step out in faith? God has a plan, and He is always willing to share His plans with us. He reveals His way to us through the truth of His written Word. We can trust Him and believe what He says more than what the surrounding circumstances are telling us. We ignore that voice of mediocrity that is telling us to settle for the status quo. No matter how loud that voice tries to anchor us to the existing state of our lives, we choose to push through and emerge into the people we were created to be. With God's help, we can reach unknown realms of possibility in life. God's definition of a full life is so much more substantial than our limited perspectives would allow us to see. Thankfully, we don't have to try and figure it all out on our own. God is with us, and He teaches us to live the life He promised.

Acknowledgments

God—My Lord and Savior, Jesus Christ, thank you for seeing beyond the surface of my life to the deep places of my heart and loving me with your grace. Every day, I depend on the Holy Spirit to lead me on your path of freedom to a fulfilled life. My heart is forever yours.

Kurt—You are my life-long love and partner in life. Thank you for believing in me when I didn't believe in myself. You are genuine, and I truly respect the man you are. I am blessed to be your wife and walk through the adventures of life with you!

Nic—Son, you inspire me with your steadfast perseverance. Whether it's running a marathon or facing the challenges of life, you endure with hope and diligence. Thank you for your continued support and encouragement throughout my writing journey. I will always be amazed that God let me be your mom.

Katie—My sweet daughter, your gentleness combined with your tenacity is a true gift. I have gleaned so much from the Lord by watching you so beautifully live out your faith. Thank you for your words of love and affirmation; they touched my heart during moments I needed them the most. I am so thankful that God let me be your mom.

Jonathan—You are, and always will be, my favorite son-in-law! Thank you for your servant's heart. Your joy and zeal for life is genuine and contagious! You are a true blessing to our family.

Wesley—My awesome grandson, you bring so much joy! Before you came to us, there was a void in our family's heart that could only be filled by you. Your Nana loves you!

My grandbaby on the way—You will soon be making your debut. I can't wait to meet you and hold you! Your Nana already loves you!

Carli Broadbent—You bring such sweetness to our family. Thank you for your cheerful smiles and loving encouragement.

Andrea Marckley—My F.A.A.T., sister, prayer partner, and friend at all times. Your decades of prayers, endless support, and input have walked me through many seasons of life and were monumental in bringing this book to fruition. You are a gift from God to me.

Matthew Barnett—You have been so much more than a wonderful pastor to our family; you have been the ultimate encourager. Over the years, I have watched you joyfully lead, inspire, and love people. I have learned so much about serving God and others through your life-changing example. Thank you for all you do.

Caroline Barnett—It's been over a decade since you first told me that I should write a book. You saw this potential inside of me long before I ever did. In spite of all my ups and downs, you remained a constant voice of faith and inspiration. Thank you for your grace and love. I admire you and treasure our friendship.

Merrilee Kaszacs—You never let me quit, and we both know there were a few times I came really close. You have seen me through a lot of tough times, and your wisdom has always challenged me to persevere. Thank you for being a true friend and confidant. I adore you, my sweet friend.

Christine Avanti-Fischer—With your powerful prayers, you faithfully spoke life over me and this book. Thank you for always believing in me, reassuring me, and breathing hope into this writing and publishing project. You helped me overcome insecurity and find the confidence that I needed to step out of the boat. I cherish you and our friendship.

Katelyn Elliott—Your heart for God and love for people shines beautifully in everything you do. Every day, I watch you serve God with dedication and commitment. Thank you for all you do behind the scenes and for always keeping a joyful spirit when you do it.

Anastasia Diamond—Mom, you have already entered into the complete fulfillment of life on the other side of eternity, and you are forever safe in the arms of heaven. I miss you now, but I will see you again.

Paul and Koral Newman—Dad and Mom, you have always been so faithful and hard working. Thank you for consistently being there with love throughout every season of my life.

Ed and Susan Jurado—You have always loved and accepted me as your own. Thank you.

Mike and Dennis—My brothers, continue to discover your dreams. I pray you both live a truly fulfilled life. Thank you for years of memories and love.

My Dream Center family—You are changing the world one person at a time, one need at a time. It is my privilege to serve God together with you.

About the Author

Danise Jurado has served as a pastoral counselor at Angelus Temple and The Dream Center in Los Angeles, California, under the leadership of Pastors Matthew and Caroline Barnett since 2001. She is also the director of The Dream Center Transitions Program. Danise is a gifted speaker and teacher, sharing at churches, speaking at conferences, and faithfully teaching a weekly women's Bible study at The Dream Center. She is passionate about encouraging and equipping people to reach their most fulfilled life in Christ. Throughout fifteen years of ministry, she has cultivated the tools in this book, and they have proven to be powerful, bringing freedom to many. Danise lives in Santa Clarita, California, with her husband of twenty-eight years, Kurt Jurado. They have two beautiful adult children, Nic and Katie; a favorite son-in-law, Jonathan; an amazing grandson, Wesley; and another grandbaby on the way.

Connect with Danise:
Blog: www.danisejurado.com
Facebook: https://www.facebook.com/danise.jurado
Twitter: https://twitter.com/danisejurado
Instagram: https://instagram.com/danisejurado/
Pinterest: https://www.pinterest.com/danisejurado/

NOTES